A POCKET GUIDE TO
PEARL HARBOR
AND **FORD ISLAND** HISTORIC MILITARY SITES

A POCKET GUIDE TO

PEARL HARBOR

AND **FORD ISLAND** HISTORIC MILITARY SITES

by **MELONI COURTWAY** with **CHRIS COOK**

USS *Arizona*
Memorial

USS *Missouri*

USS *Bowfin*

Pacific Aviation
Museum

Mutual
Publishing

Cover design by Jane Gillespie
Interior design by Courtney Tomasu

First Printing, August 2014

Mutual Publishing, LLC
1215 Center Street, Suite 210
Honolulu, Hawai'i 96816
Ph: 808-732-1709 / Fax: 808-734-4094
email: info@mutualpublishing.com
www.mutualpublishing.com

Printed in South Korea

ISBN: 978-1939487-28-5
Library of Congress Control Number:
2014938659

All photography © Douglas Peebles unless otherwise noted below.
© Archives.gov: pg. 92
© Matson Navigation Company Archives: pg. 35 (both), 65 (both), 74 (both)
© Pacific Aviation Museum Pearl Harbor: pg. 19, 39, 54, 57, 59 (both), 60, 62 (top),
64, 65 (both), 67 (all), 68-70, 71 (top and bottom), 73
© Pacific Historic Sites: pg. 13
15th ASB Hickam: pg. 87
Courtesy National Archives, photo no. 80-G-41196: pg. 61 (top), pg. 83

CONTENTS

Introduction

It was a quiet Sunday morning in Oʻahu on December 7, 1941. Breezes drifted over sugarcane fields, school-age children stumbled down dirt lanes. Military men and civilian workers, enjoying a tropical weekend at one of the prettiest billets on earth, worked off Saturday night's excursions and band concerts, at the shipyards, military bases, and airfields. At 7:55 AM a surprise air raid began. Imperial Japanese Navy fighter planes and bombers began their descent over Oʻahu, and the skies turned dark. No one – especially those men and women working on the ships and docks of Pearl Harbor, the airfield at Wheeler Army air base, and the coastal navy encampment at Kāneʻohe Bay – thought their idyllic days in a tropical paradise would ever come to an end. But that day they did.

The once shallow channels of Oʻahu's Wai Nomi waterway are today the busy port waters of Pearl Harbor, with Ford Island at its center. The island is a stretch of over 400 acres and was formerly known as Mokuʻumeʻume or "Island of Strife." Ford Island became a major port when the world's navies realized its strategic value and travelers discovered this incredible land we call Hawaiʻi.

Ford Island is named for Honolulu physician Dr. Seth Porter Ford, who acquired the island in the 1860s. Overseeing the East Loch channels of Pearl Harbor, Ford Island became a U.S. Navy base when the Battleship Era came to full steam in the early 20th century. At the same time, the airfields of Ford Island began hosting military operations in the Pacific, a bevy of seaplanes along her shallow sloping shores, along with hosting visiting dignitaries and celebrities including Amelia Earhart in the days preceding her fateful last flight.

Decades after the infamous attacks on Pearl Harbor, the historical sites surrounding Ford Island bring U.S. history to life for millions of visitors each year. From the bow of the mighty USS *Missouri* to the Pacific Aviation Museum Pearl Harbor's history of flight in Hawai'i, Ford Island is history come back to life. Across the channel, the USS *Bowfin* Submarine Museum and Park exhibits strategic (and tight) operating quarters, attracting thousands of visitors, and of course the unforgettable USS *Arizona* Memorial World War II Valor in the Pacific National Monument stands in testament to our wounds from December 7, 1941. The memories of Pearl Harbor, before and after the attack, are forever memorialized on these shores.

The attacks on Pearl Harbor were aimed at causing enough damage to keep America busy repairing her Pacific fleet, thus allow-

The Admiral Clarey Bridge connects Ford Island to Mainland O'ahu. This bridge, built in 1998, replaced the ferry system which had run for decades.

ing Japan to conquer China and other nations and islands in the eastern Pacific. To that end, the Japanese succeeded: The morning of the attack over 2,400 lives were lost at Pearl Harbor and beyond, and of the eight battleships stationed at Pearl Harbor, four were sunk and one heavily damaged. But the Japanese didn't count on the attack strengthening the resolve of the American forces and people of Hawai'i nor the vigor with which they rebuilt and moved across the Pacific to counter their enemy, ultimately to victory in the Pacific. Here memories of Pearl Harbor, before and after the attack, are forever memorialized.

Today, Ford Island and Pearl Harbor are still active military bases with strategic operations underway and military families residing right alongside memorials to the unforgettable December 7, 1941, attacks. Walk the monuments surrounding Ford Island and you are taken back in time to the day thousands of young men lost their lives. Visit historical sites where history is recreated on land, by sea, and in the air. You will take home unforgettable memories of an incredible place central to the history of the United States and Hawai'i, an island home to Hawaiian chiefs and their people, World War II heroes, military families, the heritage of the U.S. Navy, Army, and Marine Corps.

Pearl Harbor's Ford Island is America's anchor to the vast Pacific, and this book will take you on a first-class tour to the Battleship *Missouri* Memorial, the Pacific Aviation Museum Pearl Harbor, the USS *Bowfin* Submarine Museum and Park, and the iconic USS *Arizona* Memorial and World War II Valor in the Pacific National Monument – all are testaments to America's strife, strength, and fortitude.

Touring the historic sites surrounding Ford Island is a must-do for all visitors to O'ahu. With this guide in hand, you are sure to catch the most important details of these four impressive memorials, plus those of other historic military sites located in and near Honolulu. So, slap on your sunscreen, fill up that water bottle. Our journey begins now.

1

Tour Information – Planning Your Day

Welcome to the historic sites of Ford Island and Pearl Harbor. Here is invaluable information for creating a perfect day for touring the sites. Going beyond the basic tour, this chapter will give you the insights needed to fully experience this historical area rich in the U.S.'s military history.

THE BASICS

This chapter shows how to purchase tickets in advance and driving directions; provides tips on planning an optimal tour schedule; gives comprehensive details on planning visits on your own to the USS *Arizona* Memorial, the USS *Missouri*, the USS *Bowfin* Submarine Museum, and the Pacific Aviation Museum Pearl Harbor; and tells how to join a group tour of the historic sites of Ford Island and Pearl Harbor. As well there is time-sav-

Entrance to the Pearl Harbor Visitor's Center.

ing advice on practical touring matters – how to get on and off Ford Island, the rules and regulations for visiting these military sites, what to wear, where to eat and shop and find an ATM; details on ADA accessibility.

» Purchasing Tickets

Tickets for all four sites can be purchased at the Pearl Harbor Visitor Center located on Kamehameha Highway west of the Honolulu International Airport past the gates to the Pearl Harbor Navy Base. Or you can buy via the websites www.pearlharborhistoricsites.org or www.recreation.gov. **Please check these websites for the most up-to-date ticket pricing information.**

» Driving Directions
Pearl Harbor Visitor Center (1 Arizona Memorial Place)

From Waikīkī

From your hotel either take the H1 Freeway heading west, or follow Ala Moana Blvd west until it merges into HI-92/Nimitz Highway. Following either of these highways, exit onto HI-99

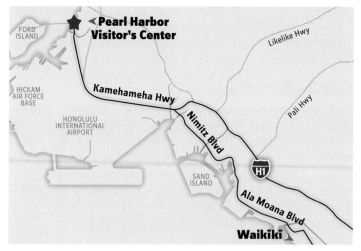

West/Kamehameha Highway towards the USS *Arizona* Memorial/Aloha Stadium. Turn left off of HI-99/Kamehameha Highway into the Pearl Harbor Visitor Center, where there are several parking lots. You may have to wait for a space if the lots are full but people are always leaving.

From Kailua/Kāne'ohe

Take the H3 Freeway heading west. Look for exit 1C and head towards the Aloha Stadium/Hālawa/Camp Smith direction. Continue straight. Turn left onto Kahupa'ani Street. Make a left onto Salt Lake Boulevard and then left onto HI-99/Kamehameha Highway. Turn right after the Ford Island Bridge exit, into the Pearl Harbor Visitor Center parking lot. Parking is found in several lots.

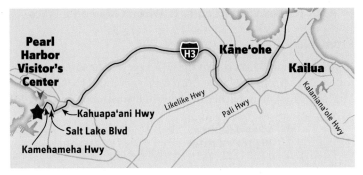

From the North Shore

From the North Shore and Wahiawa areas, take the H2 Freeway until it ends at H1 Freeway junction, heading east. Take Exit 13-B towards Hālawa Heights/Aloha Stadium. Merge briefly onto H-201 East. Take exit 1B towards Hālawa Heights/Aloha Stadium. Keep right at the fork as you pass under another freeway and follow signs to Pearl Harbor, turning left onto Kamehameha Highway. Turn right into Pearl Harbor Visitor Center. Parking is found in several lots along the property.

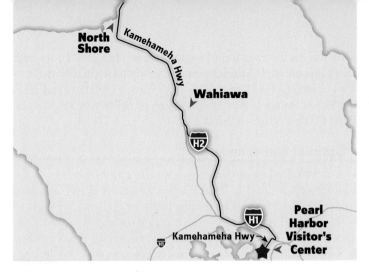

» Passport to Pearl Harbor

Adult $65, Child (4 to 12 years) $35

The Passport to Pearl Harbor is the most popular tour purchased and includes the USS *Arizona* Memorial Narrated Tour and admission to the USS *Bowfin* Submarine, Battleship *Missouri* and Pacific Aviation Museum Pearl Harbor. Passports can be purchased on www.recreation.gov or www.PearlHarborHistoricSites.org. The Passport to Pearl Harbor Tours are always available and can be easily purchased at the Pearl Harbor Visitor Center.

This two-day pass to all four historic sites is valid over a period of seven consecutive days. If you plan to see all four sites, this is your best option cost-wise. (All four sites can be done in an eight hour period).

» Half-day tours available

Adult $17.50-$30.50, Child (4 to 12 years) $11.50-$20.50

The National Park Service and the Pearl Harbor Historic Sites offer three official Pearl Harbor Half Day Tours. All three tours include the USS *Arizona* Memorial Narrated Tour plus the admission to the USS *Bowfin* Submarine, or the Battleship *Missou-*

ri or the Pacific Aviation Museum. These Half Day Tours each takes appropriately 4 to 5 hours and reservations can be made at www.PearlHarborHsitoricSites.org. These Half Day Pearl Harbor Tours are always available and can be easily purchased at the Pearl Harbor Visitor Center.

» Optimal tour schedule

It is worth the trip to just step onto the grounds of any of the historic sites located at Pearl Harbor and Ford Island. It's hard to decide which site is the best to begin or end you day with.

If possible, try to secure your USS *Arizona* Memorial Tickets early by going to www.recreation.gov or call them toll free at 1-877-444-6777. If the online tickets are sold out, do not panic, the National Park Service offers approximately 1,500 walk up tickets per day on a first come, first served basis. If you want these walk-up tickets, we recommend you go to the Pearl Harbor Visitor Center early. The Pearl Harbor Visitor Center opens daily at 7 AM (except for Thanksgiving, Christmas and New Years Day.)

Our recommendations are only a guideline. Create your own tour itinerary using the site-by-site tour pages which are designed to give you flexibility.

It is advisable in planning your tour to understand the connections between the many historic sites. They all tell a unique chapter in the big picture of the December 7, 1941, Pearl Harbor attack. Try to comprehend in advance the gravity of the events of December 7, 1941, at Ford Island and Pearl Harbor (this was "A Day That Will Live in Infamy") that took many lives given in sacrifice to our country. As well, December 7, 1941 was a day that brought the United States into World War II affecting the lives of all Americans and the destiny of our nation.

» No bags allowed! OK to bring your wallet, camera (no large camera bag), phone, and water.

Because of the sensitivity of this area, no bags may be brought along on tours of the World War II Valor in the Pacific National Monuments. This includes purses, side bags, fanny-packs, camera bags and diaper bags. Park Rangers will remind you to return them to your car. If you come by taxi or shuttle bus you can store the bag, tote, purse or camera case for $3.00. However, with proper planning, you should be able to skip this service.

Carry it all!

Clear plastic bags are allowed at the World War II Valor in the Pacific National Monument and USS *Bowfin*. Plan on carrying kids' snacks and sunscreen inside a gallon-sized Ziploc or a see-through purse.

» What to wear

Athletic shoes are a great idea and recommended out of respect either in possibly damaging the monuments or for comfort and safety in climbing ladders and staircases, as well as boarding the vessels in the tour.

We recommend a pair of shorts or pants with pockets to hold the few belongings allowed on tour. Sunglasses and a hat are also recommended because much of the day will be spent outdoors. Sunscreen should be applied before beginning the day.

» Food, gift shops and ATMs

There are two places for visitors to eat on Ford Island: The Battleship *Missouri* Memorial's outdoor food truck with its covered canteen area serves diner-style to-go food. The Laniakea Café at Pacific Aviation Museum offers excellent lunches including salads, sandwiches and grill items. The USS *Bowfin* and Valor in the Pacific National Monument have small concession stands with a more limited selection—hot dogs, chips, premade sandwiches and sodas.

All Pearl Harbor Historic Sites all have great gift stores; each store is unique and offers great military paraphernalia, WWII history books and gift items. Young and old will alike will find something interesting to memorialize their visit to Pearl Harbor. At the USS *Arizona* Memorial gift store located at the entrance of the Pearl Harbor Visitor Center, you will find gift items not available anywhere else in Hawai'i; such as U.S. flags flown over the USS *Arizona* Memorial and a Made in Hawai'i silver and gold jewelry collection featuring the "Tree Of Life" (Peace Symbol of the Pearl Harbor Visitor Center), the Sadako Crane (A International Peace Symbol) and the historic Pearl Harbor Shark Goddess. At the Pacific Aviation Museum Pearl Harbor gift store found on Ford Island, you will find unique clothing items including children's aviator jackets, retro military posters, and several books and gift items related to aviation in the Pacific. The USS *Missouri* and USS *Bowfin* Museums also have gift shops with more limited selections of historical items. We do like the battleship specific books and memorabilia found at the Missouri store however, and recommend a stop.

There are ATMs at all four stops. Debit/credit cards are accepted in all gift shops.

» ADA accessibility

The four monuments are all ADA compliant. However, the USS *Bowfin* Submarine and Battleship USS *Missouri* are naval ships, and ladders are an unavoidable reality. There is an elevator that will allow you to navigate the upper decks of the USS *Missouri*, but proceeding to most inside quarters will require some climbing and walking through raised door frames. Fortunately, the USS *Missouri's* decks offer both historical significance and unparalleled views. The USS *Bowfin* Submarine has cramped quarters, but the associated USS *Bowfin* Museum is accessible and contains valuable artifacts relating to submarine history.

» Children on tour

Children are encouraged to visit these historic sites. A few recommendations to help make their day and yours smoother.

Large bags are not allowed at most sites, so bring only the basics. Prepare to be out for many hours and calculate ahead what your younger children will need. Strollers are allowed, but you will need to store any diapers, wipes and bottles exposed and out of a bag.

Children visiting the USS *Bowfin* submarine must be at least four years old. The quarters are cramped and the equipment is delicate. In addition, the deck of the USS *Bowfin* is quite dangerous and young children are at risk of falling overboard.

The USS *Arizona* Memorial welcomes children, but please take time to help them understand the importance of respectful behavior while on tour. This site is a tomb to 900 sailors, buried at sea with their ship on December 7, 1941. It is a solemn site that requires only the best behavior—no running, yelling or throwing items while on the memorial. Younger children are welcome, too, but might enjoy this visit more from shore. Since only you know the temperament of your child, plan accordingly.

All gift shops on Ford Island and at Pearl Harbor carry a wonderful selection of child-friendly books and memorabilia. Make sure to stop in with your children to at least one shop. Browsing and touching the items is an entertaining experience for both kids and grown-ups.

THE SITES

» The USS *Arizona* Memorial – Valor in the Pacific National Monument

Open daily 7:00 AM to 5:00 PM (First tour begins at 8:00 AM, the last at 3:00 PM. Tours run every 15 minutes. Up to 150 visitors allowed on each tour.)

Tickets

All ages are free ($1.50 processing fee per/person when booked online).

Highly Recommended!

The official National Park Service USS *Arizona* Narrated Headset Tour hosted by the famous actress Jamie Lee Curtis—$7.50

This 2½-hour self guided, narrated tour provides in-depth narration of the Pearl Harbor Visitor Center's two world class exhibit halls, the "Road to War" and the "Attack" Museums. The headsets are then to be taken out to the USS *Arizona* Me-

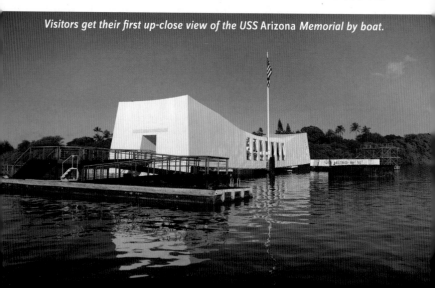

Visitors get their first up-close view of the USS Arizona *Memorial by boat.*

morial, which offer some of the best segments narrated by the Pearl Harbor Survivors and the National Park Service historians. Upon return to the Visitor Center, the Narrated Tour is then taken along the shore side to explain "The Path of Attack." The headsets can be heard in 7 languages and they even automatically translate the National Park Service's movies into the visitor's language.

Children read the names of those lost in the Pearl Harbor attacks, while visiting the Valor in the Pacific National Monument.

Let's begin with a tour of the USS *Arizona* and World War II Valor in the Pacific National Monument. The memorial to this Pennsylvania-class battleship is perhaps the most somber and poignant of the memorials. It is a main attraction for the millions of visitors who visit Hawai'i and O'ahu each year.

A Ford Island and Pearl Harbor historic sites tour is incomplete without a trip to the USS *Arizona* Memorial which floats over the remains of the sunken battleship. A visit in a boat launch to the memorial will be the main focus of your day.

The new $65 million Pearl Harbor Valor in the Pacific National Monument is operated by the National Park Service was dedicated in December of 2010. The site covers seventeen acres and is located across the inlet from Ford Island. This historic site was reconstructed on the grounds of the December 7 attacks and contains not just the USS *Arizona* Memorial and USS *Bowfin*, but three museums, points of historic interest, and gift stores. Touring Valor in the Pacific's two complimentary-admission museums helps prepare visitors for their tour of the USS

Arizona Memorial. There is no fee for entering the grounds at Pearl Harbor's Valor in the Pacific National Monument, but certain protocols must be followed upon entering—see the rules and regulations section below for details.

The USS *Arizona* Memorial tours often sell out online months in advance especially in the busy summer period. Once you know your travel dates, secure your tour times online through www.recreation.gov. The tickets are free, but there is a non-refundable $1.50 per person reservation fee.

If all the online tickets are sold out, the National Park Service offers approximately 1,500 walk-up tickets per day on a first come, first served basis. To assure you get these non-reserved tickets, you must plan to arrive at the monument by 6:30 AM the day you wish to tour as tour companies daily seek out and acquire the non-reserved tickets. This is no less of an issue in the winter months. When picking up tickets early in the morning, you may not be able to specify your tour time of choice, so be flexible in deciding in what order to visit the tour sites.

Depending on what time your USS *Arizona* tickets are booked for, you can use this guide to plan your day around the various historic sites. We like taking the tour first thing in the morning to set the scene, but there are advantages for going late in the afternoon, particularly as you can sit down to rest your tired feet.

If you have a choice of tour times, we have two recommendations: First,

Visitors board a shuttle to the floating USS Arizona *Memorial. Shuttle boats are driven by US Navy sailors, a poignant reminder of the thousands of lives lost on December 7, 1941.*

windy weather can cause the cancellation of the boat ride from a dock at the Valor in the Pacific to the USS *Arizona* Memorial. If you are buying same-day tickets, pick the earliest slot and hope the winds haven't picked up. Second, if you have a choice of several days during your trip to make this tour, watch the weather channel and avoid days with wind advisories.

If you are buying tickets weeks to months in advance (which we recommended), there is no telling what the weather will be like the day of the tour. We recommend an early morning or an afternoon tour slot (8:30 AM or 2:30 PM, for example), beginning or ending your day at Pearl Harbor with the solemn USS *Arizona* Memorial tour.

» The USS *Bowfin* Submarine and Museum
Open daily 7:00 AM to 5:00 PM

Submarine & Museum Tour

Adult $12; Child (4 to 12 years)* $5; military, senior citizens, kamaʻāina $8. (Museum only: adult $5, child $4)
Children under 4 are not permitted on the submarine for safety reasons. They may visit the museum and mini-theater at no charge.

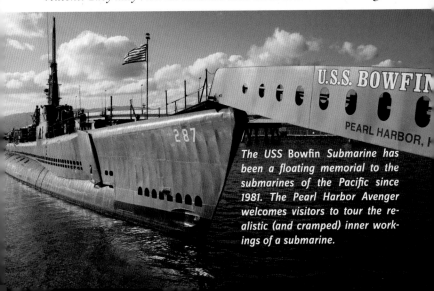

The USS Bowfin *Submarine has been a floating memorial to the submarines of the Pacific since 1981. The Pearl Harbor Avenger welcomes visitors to tour the realistic (and cramped) inner workings of a submarine.*

Audio tour offered in English, Japanese, Mandarin Chinese, and Korean.

The USS *Bowfin* Submarine Museum and Park is a self-guided (with audio headset) tour of a real Balao-class submarine that fought in the Pacific during World War II. Constructed in response to the Pearl Harbor attacks, the USS *Bowfin* would come to be known as the "Pearl Harbor Avenger," sinking dozens of enemy vessels in the Pacific (historians' claims range from 21 to 44 ships and boats sunk). Moored permanently in Pearl Harbor in 1981, the USS *Bowfin* welcomes visitors to her cramped quarters above and below decks. Here is your chance to be inside a submarine. Be advised, children under four years old are not allowed, and the conditions aboard are those of a real underwater vessel—cramped. If you are claustrophobic, or have trouble navigating narrow ladder-style staircases, we suggest you just visit the accompanying Submarine Museum adjacent to the USS *Bowfin*. There you will see interesting navy submarine paraphernalia without ever having to head inside of one. For the adventurous at heart, this stop is a must. Both the USS Bowfin Submarine and the accompanying museum provide 30-minute audio headset tours.

» The USS *Missouri* (The Mighty Mo)
Open daily 8:00 AM to 5:00 PM (June-Aug), 8:00 AM to 4:00 PM (Sept-May)

The Mighty Mo Pass
Adult $25, Child (4 to 12 years) $13
Tickets can be purchased online at USSMissouri.com, or from the main entrance to the Pearl Harbor Visitor's Center, or on Ford Island at the USS *Missouri* ticket office. Check the website for the most up-to-date information.

A regular adult pass includes your choice of one of the following tour options:
- 35-minute Mighty Mo guided tour (see below)
- Acoustiguide audio tour with headset
- Guide2Go iPod tour
- A self-guided route

The Mighty Mo Guided Tour

Included in main ticket purchase price. All ages welcome. (Highly recommended, free with regular ticket purchase)

Don't miss out on this expert-led 35-minute tour of the surrender deck as you begin your exploration of the USS *Missouri*. Walk in the footsteps of General Douglas McArthur and see firsthand where World War II officially ended. Tours are also offered with a Japanese-speaking guide. The Acoustiguide and iPod tours provide narration translations in Japanese, Korean, Chinese, and Spanish.

The USS *Missouri*, or "Mighty Mo" had her keel laid at the Brooklyn Navy Yard, eleven months and one day after the 1941 attacks on Pearl Harbor, and was therefore left unscathed, unlike the other ships bombed along Battleship Row. The USS *Missouri* went on to become the site of the Allies victory in

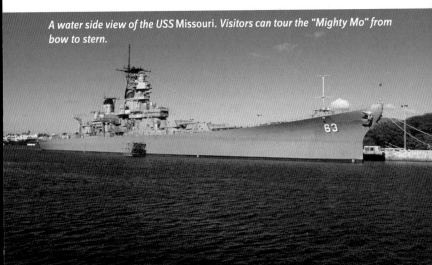

A water side view of the USS Missouri. *Visitors can tour the "Mighty Mo" from bow to stern.*

An aerial view of USS Missouri *and USS* Arizona *with Admiral Clarey Bridge in the background.*

the Pacific over Japan. She would become the site of the end of World War II in Tokyo Bay on September 2, 1945.

The Heart of the Missouri Tour: 75 minutes (strenuous)

Adult $25, Child (10 to 12 years) $12
This in-depth, expert interpretive-led tour takes hearty visitors under decks to the engineering spaces and one engine room, a place rarely visited by outsiders. We recommend tennis shoes and water bottles, and please note this is an active tour with a lot of walking. However, ship aficionados will delight in this rarely seen side of the USS *Missouri*.

Walking the ship

After you have become acquainted with the surrender deck there are several more sights worth exploring. In our Top Sites section we list our favorite moments on the USS *Missouri*, but there are hundreds more to explore as you wander the passageways.

When to go

There is no wrong time to visit the USS *Missouri*, but note that the mornings are quieter (we learned this from experts), as many visitors first head straight for the USS *Arizona* Memorial. If your USS *Arizona* tickets are later in the day, then plan your earliest stop at the USS *Missouri*. Following this book's site-by-site guide, and taking the recommended 35-minute walking tour with the docent, takes about two hours, but again the itinerary is flexible. A walk aboard the USS *Missouri* is a perfect way to work up an appetite or to walk off lunch.

» The Pacific Aviation Museum Pearl Harbor
Open daily: 9:00 AM to 5:00 PM

General Admission

Adult $25; Child (4 to 12 years) $15; Adult military or kama'āina $15; Child military or kama'āina $10

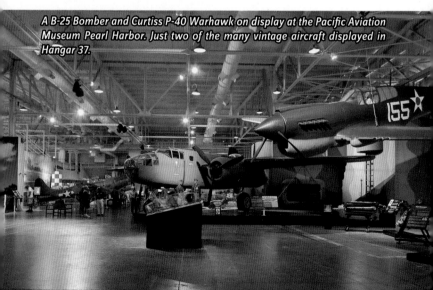

A B-25 Bomber and Curtiss P-40 Warhawk on display at the Pacific Aviation Museum Pearl Harbor. Just two of the many vintage aircraft displayed in Hangar 37.

The Aviator's Tour (two hours): Guided visit, Hangar 37 and Hangar 79

Adult $35; Child (4 to 12 years) $25; Adult military or kama'āina $25; Child military or kama'āina $20

Pacific aviation history and feats are explained in full detail during this docent-guided tour of Hangars 37 & 79 and Lt. Ted Shealy's aircraft restoration shop.

Check the website (PacificAviationMuseum.org) for the most up-to-date information.

Combat Flight Simulator

$10 for 30-minute flight and briefing (You must be seven years old to fly). Guests to Hangar 37 will be delighted to discover they don't just have to dream of flying high above the Pacific. They can soar in the Aviation Museum's Flight simulator, fighting off the enemy at Guadalcanal. Reservations recommended.

Exhibits

The Pacific Aviation Museum Pearl Harbor, located on Ford Island, opened in 2006. The museum houses dozens of exhibits focused on flight in the Pacific. From bombers to fighter jets, wooden-framed airplanes, to aviation memorials, the Pacific Aviation Museum Pearl Harbor gives a well-rounded look at Pacific aviation and a bird's-eye view of the attacks on Pearl Harbor, as well as last century life on Ford Island.

Visitors to the Pacific Aviation Museum Pearl Harbor's Hangar 37 are greeted by cheery, retro wall murals, documenting the early days of flight and travel to Hawai'i.

Lunch?

This is one of our favorite spots to stop at just about (or right before) lunchtime. Wait, didn't we say this was the Aviation Museum? We did, but they also have a great restaurant called the Laniakea Café, and it's worth trying to time your afternoon around this.

Laniakea Café is the best bet for a cool spot to eat lunch on Ford Island. Housed inside Hangar 37 at the Pacific Aviation Museum, this aviators' pit-stop serves hot plates, sandwiches, and salads daily.

The Aviation Museum also has a full well-stocked gift shop and air-conditioned Hangar 37, which makes for a break from being in the sun.

FORD ISLAND HISTORICAL TOUR BY TROLLEY

A dedicated volunteer leads this tour, providing a vast amount of knowledge about Ford Island and its inhabitants over the years. On the tour, stops are made at Ford Island memorials and plaques usually not seen by visitors. Those holding military I.D. can reserve a ticket through an MWR (Morale, Welfare, Recreation) office on O'ahu. More information can be found at www.greatlifehawaii.com/index/itt.html or by calling (808) 422-2757.

Held every third Wednesday of the month, 8:30 to 10:30 AM **Adult $25, Child (3 to 11 years) $20, Lap Child Free (2 years and under).** Limited to 25 seats per tour.

SBX RADAR

When you visit Ford Island and Pearl Harbor, you may find a rather large "pearl" floating in the waterways nearby. The U.S. Navy's Sea-Based X-Band Radar, or SBX, resembles a large white balloon floating in the Pearl Harbor waters. In reality, this advanced X-Band radar dome is mounted on a self-propelled, mobile, semi-submersible platform that can be positioned to cover any region of the globe – even in high seas

This "Pearl" in Pearl Harbor can be seen from miles around when it's in port. In reality, this large floating dome is a Sea-Based-X-Band Radar system.

and gale wind conditions. This long-range radar is a powerful tool in the United States' missile defense system and is moved around to several Pacific regions, including Alaska. If you see the SBX at Pearl Harbor, it is likely in port for repairs.

GETTING ON AND OFF FORD ISLAND

Ford Island is an active military base, and Pearl Harbor's World War II Valor in the Pacific National Monument is a sacred historical site. Be advised: There are very strict rules regulating what can and cannot be brought onto the monument and how to get on and off Ford Island.

By Shuttle Bus: All guests must park in designated parking areas near Pearl Harbor World War II Valor in the Pacific National Monument. There is limited parking, but many visitors come and go throughout the day, so finding a spot should not be a problem.

Ford Island requires a military I.D. for entrance unless you take a specified bus from Pearl Harbor (which we recommend). If you have purchased tickets to the Pacific Aviation Museum Pearl Harbor or Battleship Missouri, the shuttle ride is free. If you would only like to visit the USS *Oklahoma* memorial, the shuttle ride will cost $3. The bus runs about every 15 minutes and there is a covered shaded lanai for waiting. Please see the rules and regulations below before setting off!

By Car: If you have a military approved I.D., you can drive your vehicle onto Ford Island and park near the USS *Missouri*. Please be advised that this is an active base and a family housing area, so the utmost respect is expected of all visitors.

RULES AND REGULATIONS

Depending on when you have secured tickets for touring the USS *Arizona* Memorial, you may want to begin your day in several ways. No matter in which order you take in the four primary historic stops on this tour, you will need to park near Pearl Harbor's Valor in the Pacific National Monument (unless you have a military I.D.). From Valor in the Pacific, you will take a bus to Ford Island's USS *Missouri* and the Pacific Aviation Museum. Ask a park ranger if you need assistance finding the bus terminal. The bus system is a secure route and runs about every 15 minutes from Valor in the Pacific, stopping at both monuments on Ford Island. Just as at the USS *Arizona* Memorial and the USS *Bowfin*, no bags are allowed on the bus, so please plan accordingly. Water bottles are allowed, as are hats and wallets. Cameras must be carried without a bag, however, which makes a smartphone a great choice for maintaining communications and taking photos—as well as being small enough to fit in your pocket.

TWO

2

Ford Island History and Historic Sites

FORD ISLAND HISTORY

Today the once-shallow channels and fishponds known in old Hawai'i as Pu'uloa (long hill) and as Wai Nomi (pearl water) have become the busy, deepwater naval port of Pearl Harbor. In the center of this strategic military harbor is Ford Island. The flat, 450-plus acre island is traditionally known as Moku'ume'ume, the "Island of Strife," or as some say, the name refers to a nighttime game traditionally played on the island by Hawaiians. Local residents made up their own modern-day Hawaiian name for Ford Island, calling it Poka 'Ailana.

Ford Island came into non-Hawaiian royalty ownership over 200 years ago. In about 1810 King Kamehameha deeded Ford Island to his Spanish adviser Don Francisco de Paula Marin, who lived in the Vineyard Street area of downtown Honolulu. Marin employed the island for grazing sheep, hogs, goats and rabbits he sold to provision visiting foreign ships. A family trust of Dr. Seth Porter Ford, a Honolulu physician and the island's namesake, purchased the island in the 1860s and owned it into the early 1890s. In 1891 Ford's son sold the family's island to the prominent Ii family, who owned large blocks of land in the vicinity of Pearl Harbor. In 1899 the Oahu Sugar Company leased the island from the Ii Estate, planting about half the island in sugarcane. Harvested sugarcane was loaded onto a barge at a dock jutting off the north side of Ford Island.

This aerial photo of Ford Island looks towards Pearl Harbor, on the upper left, and the Adm. Clarey Bridge. Just to the right of the long dock pictured here you can see the remains of the USS Utah *(mostly submerged, and brown with rust).*

As American involvement in World War I grew, the first military facilities were installed on the island. Two gun batteries were built on Ford Island to defend Pearl Harbor, placed on two parcels of land purchased from the Ii family. In 1916 the use of Ford Island as an airfield for flying boats was recommended by a military pilot sent to Hawai'i by the War Department. In 1917 the War Department took over the sugar-growing leases and negotiated purchase of Ford Island from the Ii family for use by the army and the navy. By 1919 the Army Air Service's Luke Field was in use, located on the west ('Ewa) side of Ford Island and named for World War I ace army fighter pilot Frank Luke, who was killed on the "western front." Luke Field became a self-contained army air base. In 1923 the navy joined the ranks at Ford Island, establishing Naval Air Station Pearl Harbor on the east (Diamond Head) side of the island. The shallow, sloping waters surrounding Ford Island were perfect for seaplane landings, a frequent sight in those times. Ferry service then provided easy and regular access between the island and Pearl Harbor Naval Station, carrying passengers and motor vehicles.

By 1935 several dozen army bombers were stationed on Ford Island, making the island too tight a fit for both army and navy operations. Soon a swap of mainland airfields paved the way for Ford Island to be occupied by just the navy. The army then began purchasing land to the east of Pearl Harbor to construct its Hickam Field, which was opened for Army Air Corps flights in 1940.

Overseeing the East Loch channels of Pearl Harbor, Ford Island would soon be the centerpiece of the harbor when the Age of the Battleship came to full steam in the pre-World War II era, the huge ships tying up along its east shore.

PEARL HARBOR NAVAL STATION HISTORY

East of Ford Island, across the inlet, Hawai'i's King David Kalākaua deeded the site of today's Pearl Harbor naval base and shipyard in 1887 to the United States War Department for military occupation as a "coaling and repair station" for navy vessels and American merchant ships. In trade, President Grover Cleveland and Congress lowered tariffs on Hawaiian sugar shipped to the Mainland, providing a huge boost to the sugar industry in Hawai'i. The navy named the base Pearl Harbor after the *momi* (pearls) found in the mother-of-pearl shells that once grew in abundance in its deep waters.

However, while the inner waters of Pearl Harbor were deep enough, the shallow-draft entrance at the mouth of the Pearl Harbor estuary blocked entrance of deep-water naval vessels such as battleships. In 1899, once Hawai'i became a territory of the United States, the navy established a base on the east side of the harbor and began dredging the harbor entrance. The first large navy warship crossed the harbor entrance in 1911.

Meanwhile, a battleship-size drydock and other shipyard facilities were being built at Pearl Harbor.

By December 1941, the Pearl Harbor Naval Base was a major international military port, with anchorage for dozens of ships, a major ship repair yard, a submarine base, and huge fuel storage facilities.

The morning of the Pearl Harbor attack, the bulk of the U.S. Pacific Fleet lay at anchor here. Along "Battleship Row" just offshore of Ford Island's east shore, berthed stem to stern, were the USS *Arizona, Nevada, Tennessee, Maryland, West Virginia, Oklahoma,* and *California.* Among other ships at anchor nearby were the cruisers *Detroit* and *Raleigh* and the seaplane tender *Tangier.*

The airfield at Ford Island was filled with navy scout and patrol planess grouped closely together like sitting ducks when the Japanese surprise attack began. The navy had built up their aircraft facilities on Ford Island leading up to the attack, sta-

An aerial photo of Pearl Harbor with Ford Island in the distance. The Adm. Clarey Bridge can be seen on the far left.

tioning PBY flying boats and a wide range of other naval airplanes. Some 33 naval aircraft were destroyed on the ground at Ford Island during the attack.

Thankfully, many of the navy's carrier-based planes were at sea the morning of the December 7 attack, taking part in exercises aimed at combating just such an event. It was the absence of the carrier planes that led to confusion in identifying incoming planes the morning of the attack. Upon the carrier-based planes return following the attack, these surviving pilots and planes provided vital support for Oʻahu in the days of uncertainty following December 7, a time when many feared the Japanese attacks would resume.

In a rapid, pivotal response to the December 7, 1941, attacks, Admiral Chester W. Nimitz was selected ten days later as Commander in Chief of the United States Pacific Fleet (CINCPAC). He took command at Pearl Harbor on December 31. Though a change-of-command ceremony at Pearl Harbor usually took place aboard a fleet battleship, there were none to be found, all sunk or too badly damaged for the event. Instead, the ceremony took place aboard the USS *Grayling* (SS-209), a Tambor-class submarine that escaped the wrath brought down on Pearl Harbor, arriving December 17. Nimitz successfully undertook the daunting task of organizing and rebuilding the Pacific fleet to halt the Japanese advance.

During World War II, Ford Island served as a naval aircraft sentinel for the Pearl Harbor Naval Base. Following the war, the air base at Ford Island gradually became obsolete with the arrival of modern aircraft, and in 1962 it was deactivated by the navy.

Ford Island airfield hosted visiting non-military dignitaries and celebrities, too, including Amelia Earhart in the days preceding her fateful last flight across the Pacific in 1937.

Today Ford Island is home to hundreds of military families while remaining a working navy base. The National Oceanic Atmospheric Administration's (NOAA) Daniel K. Inouye Pacific Regional Center is now operating there, too. Because of this, security concerns require a guard to check if visitors have the military I.D. needed to self-escort their vehicle onto the island. Visitors, and military personnel and families, are expected to treat this spot with the utmost respect as Ford Island is a living and working monument to a great tragedy in U.S. history.

Along with touring the well-known USS *Missouri* and Pacific Aviation Museum Pearl Harbor, guests to Ford Island can visit the USS *Oklahoma* Memorial, which is located just before the entrance to the "Mighty Mo." Guests holding military I.D. are allowed to take a self-guided tour of the USS *Utah* Memorial*. Please note that the shuttle bus does not stop here. The USS *Utah* sank in place on the opposite, west side of Ford Island from the USS *Arizona* and rests quietly there today with 58 men and one young girl's remains entombed.

*The USS *Utah* was in use as a training vessel in 1941.

VISITING FORD ISLAND SITES

» Admiral Clarey Bridge

Not many visitors driving over the Admiral Clarey Bridge to Ford Island know that prior to 1998 travelers to Ford Island

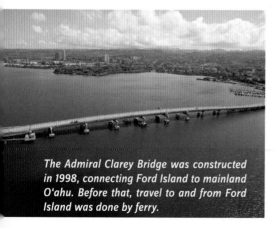

The Admiral Clarey Bridge was constructed in 1998, connecting Ford Island to mainland Oʻahu. Before that, travel to and from Ford Island was done by ferry.

from mainland Oʻahu needed to ride on a navy-run ferry for transport across the Pearl Harbor inlet. Then only military families who resided on the island and their invited guests, and working military and civilian personnel, could take the trip aboard one of two motor-vehicle ferries, or one of several passengers-only ferries. This has changed now that the floating drawbridge named for Admiral Bernard "Chick" Clarey (a submarine commander during World War II, and in the early 1970s Commander in Chief, U.S. Pacific Fleet) is open providing secure passage for hundreds of vehicles a day (and night). Prior to the Clarey Bridge being built, anyone who missed the last ferry of the evening, departing at 11 PM, found themselves landlocked on either side.

THE USS *OKLAHOMA* (BB-37)

With so many lives lost aboard the USS *Arizona* on December 7, 1941, adjacent battleships such as the USS *Oklahoma* are often remembered only for being sunk that fearful day. But the USS *Oklahoma* had spent a long tour of duty at sea prior to arriving in Pearl Harbor in 1937. Since her commissioning in 1916, she toured Europe and took part in naval exercises off Cuba, among other duties. The USS *Oklahoma* was side-by-side with the USS *Maryland* when Japanese navy torpedoes and aerial fire rained down. Men of the USS *Oklahoma* who made it overboard alive clamored aboard the USS *Maryland* to fire back at the attacking planes above. Within 12 minutes, however, the USS *Oklahoma* listed, tilting so far that her masts touched bottom, 429 men going down with her.

Like most of the ships

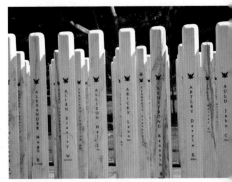

Marble pillars represent the 429 sailors killed on or near the USS Oklahoma on December 7, 1941. Walking through these man-sized monuments is a striking reminder of the lives lost in WWII at Pearl Harbor.

The USS Oklahoma *Memorial is a must-see for visitors to Ford Island. This poignant landmark is situated just before the guest entrance to the USS Missouri.*

sunk or damaged in the Pearl Harbor attacks, the USS *Oklahoma* was righted by 1943, but the damage to her hull was so great she could only be sold for scrap, a remarkably sad ending to the career of such a noble ship. Indeed, almost in protest, the USS *Oklahoma* after the war sank at sea in a storm about 500 miles east of Hawai'i while being towed to a scrap yard in Oakland. Today the marble memorial to the USS *Oklahoma*, erected in 2007 on Ford Island, is a poignant site and one worth walking through on your way to the USS *Missouri*, which is now berthed where the USS *Oklahoma* once moored.

How to find it

The USS *Oklahoma* Memorial is found just outside the USS *Missouri's* front gates. Please take time to enter its marble pillars, which are each inscribed with the name of one of the 429 sailors and Marines lost on December 7.

THE USS *UTAH* (BB-31)

Though the USS *Utah* left naval service as a battleship by 1941, she was active the day of the Pearl Harbor attack as an anti-air-craft gunnery training vessel. Sadly, her fate would be just that when Japanese aircraft struck her with a deadly blow at 8:01 AM on December 7. The first of two torpedoes to strike the USS *Utah* caused her to list to one side as men rushed to escape. On board was Chief Watertender Peter Tomich, one of the many winners of the Congressional Medal of Honor from that day. Unfortunately, Tomich would not live to receive his award; instead, he perished aboard the USS *Utah* while ensuring as many men as possible could escape the sinking ship before him.

Soon after she sank, rescuers outside the USS *Utah* could hear the knocking and banging of sailors trapped inside, desperately calling out for help. A cutting torch was secured from the nearby cruiser *Raleigh*, and four men were rescued from her hull. Sixty-four men died aboard the USS *Utah* that day. To this day, many of the 461 USS *Utah* survivors choose to have their ashes interred in the waters of Pearl Harbor, rejoining their shipmates lost aboard the USS *Utah*.

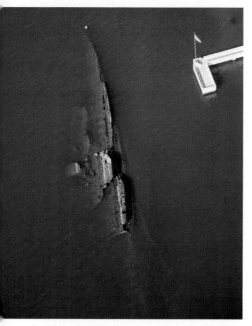

The USS Utah *remains where she sank off the northwest side of Ford Island. Depending on the tide, visitors can sometimes glimpse portholes that emerge above the waterline.*

Baby Wagner's ashes onboard the USS *Utah* when it sank

Chief Yeoman Robert Wagner had the misfortune of losing not one, but two daughters in infancy during his time in the navy: the first, Helen Wagner, in 1936. Helen's ashes he spread at sea. The second daughter, Nancy Lynne Wagner, was a twin born prematurely, who had not survived. The grieving father planned to also spread her ashes at sea when a chaplain could be assigned to the USS *Utah*. Before that could happen, however, the Japanese attack on Pearl Harbor would sink the USS *Utah*, taking with her the fifty-eight crew members entombed in the waters of Pearl Harbor, and the remains of Wagner's daughter. Nancy Lynne is the only female buried at sea with the wrecks of December 7, 1941.

The remains of the USS Utah *can be viewed from this walkway on the north side of Ford Island. A plaque tells visitors about the only baby to be interred from the Pearl Harbor attack, those of Baby Wagner, a child whose ashes were due to be scattered at sea but instead rest in the shallow waters here with many sailors alongside her. Visitors to the USS* Utah *must have a military I.D. or an escort.*

How to find it

The USS *Utah* Memorial is surrounded by military housing, so visitors are asked to show the utmost respect for the residents' privacy when entering the area. To locate the memorial, follow Yorktown Boulevard and take a right towards the flag marking Memorial. Park near the memorial, not by the adjacent housing. Military I.D. is required to visit the USS *Utah* Memorial. The shuttle does not stop near this memorial.

HANGAR 6

The first strike on December 7, 1941, came at 7:55 AM that Sunday morning when Japanese Zero pilot Kakuichi Takahashi misread a signal, dropping his payload directly on Ford Island's Hangar 6, instead of on one of the targeted battleships moored just yards away. Navy First Class Ted Croft was on duty, just five minutes from retiring for the day, when the bombs hit. He would become the first casualty of the Pearl Harbor attacks, and unbelievably the only casualty from that day on Ford Island. Visitors to the island with military I.D. are permitted to walk the area near where Hangar 6 once stood, about 200 yards east of the Aviation Museum. In the pavement you will still find blast marks from the attack, but not much else.

LUKE FIELD AND AMELIA EARHART

The world's spotlight was on Ford Island and Luke Field long before the attacks on December 7. The one and only Amelia Earhart made several takeoffs and landings from this historic airstrip during her flying time in the islands, often en route to breaking a record. Earhart is the first woman to win the Distinguished Flying Cross, awarded to her in 1932, and the first person to fly solo from Hawai'i to California, accomplished in 1935.

Amelia Earhart took the world by storm as she began to make transoceanic flights in the pioneering years of aviation. It was at Ford Island's Luke Field that Amelia's first attempt at a round-the-world flight came to a halt. In March 1937 she had commuted her Lockheed Electra 10E from Wheeler Field in Central O'ahu to Ford Island, because of the favorable trade winds blowing there. The plane became damaged on a takeoff attempt at Luke Field, blowing out a tire, compromising her landing gear. This sidelined Earhart's round-the-world record attempt for many months before her next try, which ended with a mysterious disappearance in the Pacific that is still being investigated today with great interest worldwide in finding her lost airplane.

Forced to quit when her right landing tire is blown out, Amelia's round-the-world flight is canceled.

Amelia back again in Hawai'i for her round-the-world flight, where she takes off from Luke Field, March 18-20, 1937.

FORD ISLAND HISTORIC HOUSING AND THE JOHN WAYNE HOUSE

As you cross the Admiral Clarey Bridge to Ford Island and curve round the turning circle, you will notice lovely historic homes to your left. This is the neighborhood referred to as Nob Hill, still home to circa 1920s officers housing and located in one of the more picturesque settings found on earth. During the attacks on Pearl Harbor, this housing area became ground zero for medical triage and emergency care of sailors crawling from the burning waters to Ford Island's shores. Nob Hill families used their own linens and alcohol to provide first aid. Families were stranded at Nob Hill for three days with little to no resources available for evacuation. Children and spouses banded together, carrying for each other and watching the skies for any new attacks. The USS *Arizona*, moored just feet away from these homes, crushed Ford Island's water supply when she sank, forcing residents to use swimming pool water for drinking water, for washing, and wound cleaning.

Rows of Chief Petty Officer housing located on Ford Island were in the direct line of fire when the Japanese attacks occurred. Many of these smaller houses have been demolished, or are condemned, but one house, "Building 30," has survived thanks in great part to Hollywood. In the 1965 film *In Harm's Way*, John Wayne played Captain Rockwell W. "Rock" Torrey. Torrey's fictional house was staged in Building 30. For the filming, workers relocated the house to the picturesque Nob Hill housing area. Building 30 still stands today amid more senior officer housing, on the point looking out between the USS *Arizona* Memorial and the Admiral Clarey Bridge. The CPO quarters are small in comparison to those of its officer housing counterparts, so Building 30 is a unique moment in time captured forever on film and now under restoration as a historic residence.

Newer homes can be found on the eastern end of Ford Island, while historic homes are located in the upper right of this photo and to the upper left. Several houses on Ford Island have survived the years since WWII including the house used by John Wayne in the movie In Harm's Way, *a cozy 1920s bungalow, which has been restored and is still used as a residence.*

The Nob Hill houses are best viewed from near the USS *Oklahoma* Memorial, or by looking inland from the dock of the USS *Missouri*. The homes are active residences, so self-touring the area is not recommended, especially if you do not have a military I.D.

Across the street from the USS *Utah* Memorial you will also see bungalow-style historic homes. They are occupied by working military families today, and it is respectfully requested that visitors do not approach the residents.

THREE

The USS *Missouri* (BB-63)

Iowa-Class Battleship - Commissioned 1944, New York

Built in New York and Christened on January 29, 1944 at the Navy Yard at Brooklyn, the USS *Missouri*, or "Mighty Mo" as she is fondly nicknamed, arrived in the Pacific Theater in time for the close of World War II. Construction of her massive 887-foot hull was a monument to American military strength when she was commissioned in 1944, though in strategic importance the navy's battleships were then giving way to the aircraft carrier. But the Mighty Mo did see action when America took the fight west across the Pacific to Japan, bombing Japanese forces during the battles of Okinawa and Iwo Jima.

The USS *Missouri* is famous for being the ship chosen for the signing of the Japanese surrender document by representatives of the nine Allied forces and a representative of Japan. The momentous signing took place in Tokyo Bay on September 2, 1945, on the forward end of the superstructure, adjacent to Turret #2, on the 01 level veranda deck, starboard side. Now known as the Surrender Deck, it was here on the USS *Missouri* that the Japanese government would concede its power to the Allied Forces with nearly 260 ships waiting in the waters nearby.

After the USS *Missouri's* successful first tour, and the surrender of Japan, she would go on to fight for the U.S. Navy in the Korean War in the early 1950s before joining the mothball

The USS Missouri *stands guard over the USS* Arizona *Memorial in the waters of Pearl Harbor.*

ball fleet for 30 years. Recommissioned and modernized under President Reagan, the Mighty Mo would enter the Persian Gulf in 1987 and 1991, and by the end of her career would hold 11 battle stars for service in WWII, the Korean War, and Operation Desert Storm (proof of which you can look for on your tour). In 1998, the USS *Missouri* was donated to the USS *Missouri* Memorial Association and took up residence as a living museum on the pier F-5 on Ford Island in Pearl Harbor. Today, thousands of visitors walk the decks of the USS *Missouri* each week, exploring a war machine from decades gone by. Look closely as you tour and you may recognize location scenes from modern movies and television shows filmed aboard the USS *Missouri*, a ship which continues to inspire those from Hollywood and beyond.

With your purchase of tickets for the USS *Missouri* tour comes a complimentary 35-minute guided walking tour of the main decks. This tour is optional, but we highly recommend it to start off your visit. After getting acquainted with the USS

Missouri guided by a dedicated docent, you can branch off on your own to explore the rest of this monumental ship.

Let's start on the USS *Missouri's* main deck, her teak wood planks stretching out around you on all sides, and the O1 level, one deck up, Welcome to the Mighty Mo.

MAIN DECK

» Teak Decks

We can't underestimate the functional importance of the miles of teak-wood decking lining the outside walks of the Mighty Mo. Looking down at your feet, you'll notice a highway of history inlaid below them. Ships the world over have their decks lined in this mold and fire resistant wood. In addition to a guaranteed long life, teak wood is the perfect insulator. Hours of exposure to the Pacific sun would quickly heat the interior of the USS *Missouri* were it not for the thick insulation of this wood planking above. During the height of World War II, while the Mighty Mo sailed the Pacific,

Miles of teak decking line main decks of the Mighty Mo. Restoration is helping to preserve this unique and beautiful element of maritime history.

her decks were painted a gray-blue color, as were all the horizontal surfaces. This blended the USS *Missouri* in with the deep blue ocean so enemy pilots flying overhead would fail to spot her. Salt water and age have taken their toll on some of the original decking. Today the decks are being restored to their original glory, section-by-section; on your tour you may see volunteers doing some of the work.

» The Kamikaze Deck

While in battle on April 11, 1945, off of Okinawa, Japan, one of the most costly battles of World War II for the U.S. Navy, the U.S. Navy Fleet came under attack by several Japanese aircraft. The USS *Missouri* would be struck twice, but despite this would suffer little significant damage.

One of the more emotionally charged displays aboard the USS *Missouri* is also one of the least dramatic in appearance, but absolutely worthy of your attention. The Kamikaze Deck (main deck level), found along her starboard side can be found by looking for footprints that mark the location where a Marine Guard, bugler, the pallbearers and the Chaplain stood during the burial of the Japanese pilot found on board the USS *Missouri* after his Zero broke apart at impact, spilling wing wreckage onto the ship and starting a fire on an upper level. Visitors can look over the side to view a dent left when the Japanese pilots plane made contact with the USS *Missouri*.

Captain at the time, William

The infamous Mitsubishi A6M2 Zero would become the symbol of Japanese kamikaze attacks during WW II.

M. Callaghan ordered a burial at sea with Japanese flag and three-volley rifle salute fired by marines aboard. Indeed, standing at this post today you can imagine the young men who gave their lives, and the resulting impact on their families, of those who fought on both sides of this war. Perhaps the Japanese Pilot's fight wasn't on the right side of history, but this spot marks the place where Captain Callaghan gave a touch of humanity to both sides of the war.

» Officers Ward Rooms and Gallery

We recommend saving a visit to the USS *Missouri's* ward room and museum for after your below-decks tour (a description of below decks follows this section). Your lower-decks tour exits into this area, providing a nice chance for you to sit down and take in some of what you've seen. In 2014 this area of the ship is under restoration.

Entering this main-deck interior area, you find the living quarters of the USS *Missouri's* officers. Officers, as naval tradition dictates, had more spacious cabins in general, and the obvious distinction of portholes, a luxury on this ship known for its hot interior during a Pacific tour. Dining for officers was more formal than service below decks, and being able to relax in their well-appointed officers' lounge must have looked alluring to enlisted men. Make sure to stop at the glass-encased replica of the USS *Missouri* that portrays how the ship looked on arrival in the Pacific.

GUN DECK AND TURRETS

» 16-inch Turrets

There is no denying that perhaps the most prominent features of the exterior of the USS *Missouri* are her three massive 16-inch triple-gun turrets, two turrets forward, one aft. With gun barrels replaced just before the Korean War, each turret is capable of firing a shell that creates a crater 30 feet across, and has a range of up to 26 miles. A barrage from the USS *Missouri* guns can obliterate a football-field size area with great accuracy. Each projectile weighs nearly 2,700 pounds. Empty shells from the 16-inch guns can be seen as you enter the USS *Missouri* from

There is no denying the enormity of the USS Missouri's 16-inch turrets. Towering above visitors, they are a focal point while on tour. With a range of up to 26 miles, the USS Missouri's turrets require a complex set of maneuvers and dozens of sailors to be fired.

the dock (you may have even posed for a photo in front of one). Not only could this ship fire these behemoth rounds 26 miles, attacking enemy forces out of line of sight, she could do so every 30 seconds, firing by aiming these guns off the port or starboard sides of the ship. This was no small feat, and required a crew of up to 110 hands to orchestrate the delicate ballet of loading, and reloading, each turret. Extending several decks deep into the ship, each turret contained five levels of operation, and machinery specially designed to hoist and load the massive shells, elevate and fire them. At Gun Turret 3, on the main deck, you can climb a short ladder into the belly of the beast as it were, to see what the inner operations of such a large gun look like.

» Twin Gun Mounts

Armament the rest of the ship, to protect the USS *Missouri* from more immediate and direct danger from nearby ships and coastal batteries, are five twin-gun mounts (ten total smaller guns) with 5-inch guns, capable of firing 55-pound rounds over 9 miles and 35,000 feet up in the air. It was with

Twin gun mounts on the Mighty Mo were critical in fending off kamikaze attacks.

these guns that the USS *Missouri's* sailors fought off the hordes of kamikaze planes in the Okinawa attacks, taking down eleven.

» Anti-Aircraft Guns

Also protecting the USS *Missouri* from direct danger are mounted on her decks twenty 40-millimeter quad guns and forty-nine 20-millimeter anti-aircraft guns. The 50-caliber long-barrel machine guns mounted at intervals around the outside perimeter of the ship today, are authentic de-militarized weapons of the type that were installed in those locations at the time the ship was modernized. The single 40-mm quad mount displayed on the pier is an authentic weapon that was removed from the USS *Missouri* when mothballed in 1955, and was recovered for pier display in recent years.

» Weapon Modernization

The bridge and upper decks of the USS Missouri *were modernized in 1986, including the addition of a Combat Engagement Center and modern sea warfare weapons.*

When the USS *Missouri* was brought back to life in 1986 under President Reagan, her overhaul included the obvious need for modernized weapons. Tomahawk missiles were brought on board for sea-to-land attack, harpoon missiles were mounted to fight enemy vessels at sea, and close-in weapons, Gatling guns, replaced the original 40-millimeter and 20-millimeter guns for better accuracy fighting faster modern planes and jets. See our section on the Combat Engagement Center (CEC) to better understand modernization of the USS *Missouri*.

THE 01 LEVEL

» The Surrender Plaque and Instruments of Surrender: September 2, 1945 - Tokyo Bay

As Japan's defeat became clear, an international stage was set for surrender aboard the USS *Missouri*. Taking into careful account the cultural significance of this moment, the Japanese sent a 11-man delegation aboard the USS *Missouri* for the signing. Signing the actual surrender were Foreign Minister Mamoru Shigemitsu, a civilian representing the emperor of Japan and Japanese government, and General Yoshijiro Umezu from the Japanese Imperial Army. Representing the United States was (in order of significance) General Douglas MacArthur, as supreme commander for the Allied forces, Fleet Admiral Chester W. Nimitz representing the United States, General Hsu Yung-Chang representing the Republic of China, Admiral Sir Bruce Fraser representing the United Kingdom, Lieutenant General Kuzma Nikolaevich Derevyanko for the Union of Soviet Socialist Republics, General Sir Thomas Blamey for the Commonwealth of Australia, Colonel Lawrence Moore Cosgrove for Canada, General Jacques LeClerc for the French Republic, Admiral C.E.L. Helfrich representing the Kingdom of the Netherlands, and Vice Marshall Leonard M. Isitt for the Dominion of New Zealand. As Japan is west of the International Dateline, for those on board in Tokyo Harbor the date was September 2; for those in Hawai'i and in the mainland United States, the date was still September 1, 1945, as news of the official end of World War II went out over radio waves, marking the sixth anniversary of Hitler ordering his army to invade Poland, thus starting World War II.

Written into History

Great care was taken in orchestrating this historical day, and no detail was overlooked. The USS *Missouri's* Commanding officer, Captain Stuart Murray realized the table intended for the signing ceremony, provided by the British, was too small to hold the two surrender documents. A wardroom table was first sought, without remembering that all the wardroom tables are bolted to deck. He then ordered a folding mess table from the enlisted mess brought forward, and covered that with a green baise tablecloth from the wardroom. MacArthur's wife had gifted him a pen manufactured by the Parker Pen Company of Wisconsin, one that would come to symbolize the end of war after the signing of surrender. To commemorate the event, the Parker Pen Company produced 1,945 pens identical to MacArthur's.

A bronze statue of Admiral Chester W. Nimitz stands a welcoming duty post at the entrance to the Battleship Missouri Memorial.

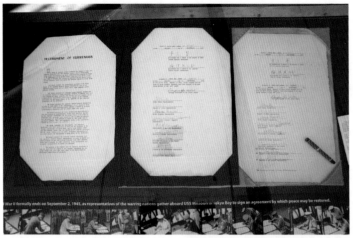

The Instruments of Surrender, signed by Allied forces and Japanese represen-tatives, ending WWII in the Pacific, can be viewed aboard the USS Missouri.

"Your Signature Here"

On your tour of the USS *Missouri*, standing between the sur-render plaque and the glass-encased Instruments of Surrender, turn towards the Pacific and look out. Imagine ships from na-tions the world over sailing in to witness their representatives at the signing. Now, imagine the stress that might cause for a participant. Surrounded by admirals and captains, Canadi-an Colonel Lawrence Moore Cosgrove mistakenly signed his name a line below where he ought to on the official Instrument of Surrender document. To this day, the first document has a blank space, and a curious array of signatures below it, as each signee to follow skipped down a line. Colonel Cosgrove was carefully guided through the next signing, so of course the sec-ond document in the surrender case is perfectly done. No one seemed worse for the wear, and Cosgrove's mistake only adds to the unique history of the surrender aboard the USS *Missouri*.

Surrender Plaque

The Surrender Plaque inlaid in the forward 01 level veranda deck adjacent to the Captain's cabin of the USS *Missouri* marks the exact spot where the surrender documents were signed. Note the longitude and latitude listed. The positions were documented at exactly 9 AM the morning of September 2, 1945, when the USS *Missouri's* navigators took a precise fix on her location. They then cut the electrical power to her gyrocompasses, locking this location in history. The plaque reads: Latitude 35 degrees, 2' 17" North – Longitude 139 degrees 45' 36" East.

The Surrender Plaque, mounted in the USS Missouri's *teak decking, marks the exact location of surrender ceremonies on September 2, 1945.*

Commodore Perry's Flag

As you stand outside the captain's quarters on deck 01, notice Commodore Perry's flag above the Surrender Deck. Perry's flag represents the beginning of America's history with Japan. The flag is a replica of the actual flag carried ashore by Commodore Matthew C. Perry, having sailed his "Black Ships" into Tokyo Bay to negotiate with Japan, opening trade with the nation for the first time after years of self-imposed isolation. The symbolism of the Perry Flag was important to the surrender in 1945. At special request of General MacArthur, the historic flag was brought on board for the surrender ceremonies.

Many a visitor has questioned the direction of this flag, with its stars on the right and stripes jutting out to the left. Is it backwards? The flag is actually backwards because the reverse side of the original flag had been protected with a backing of white linen; so there was only one viewable side to display. The replica reproduces that display.

Commodore Perry's Flag, an exact replica of the 1853 flag flown above American ships sailing into Japan, and again flown above the surrender ceremonies in Tokyo Bay.

UPPER LEVELS

Combat Engagement Center – Level 02
– 1984 Modernization

The Combat Engagement Center (CEC) was the heart of the ship's operations after modernization. Here, sailors would execute strategic wartime communications and mapping. Top photo: radar screens. Bottom photo: trained sailors could write backwards on these glass screens, allowing those in charge to read them from the other side.

The Combat Engagement Center, known on board as the CEC, was installed during the modernization of the USS *Missouri*, after her stint in the mothball fleet. The CEC is housed in the former flag quarters and was designed to meet the growing technological needs of sea warfare, adding advanced radar systems, plotting and communication equipment. Her crew trained to operate these specialized devices from inside the darkened strategic operations center of the ship. A visit today gives you a glimpse of the intense environment crewmen at war would work under. The USS *Missouri* staff asks that visitors please not touch the sensitive equipment still housed within.

The Bridge and Observation Deck – Level 04 and 05

Standing just above the enclosed bridge, the Flying Bridge offers a windy, but worthwhile, view. Rest your hands on the exposed navigation equipment and feel the inner rumbling of the ship. Imagine looking out past her bow as the Mighty Mo navigated through the Panama Canal after her commissioning, during the War in the Pacific, in the waters of the Persian Gulf, and returning home to Pearl Harbor in 1998 to stand watch over the remains of the USS *Arizona*. This view

A docent guides visitors outside the CEC. The bridge, seen in the upper left of the photo, can be self-toured.

from here is in our opinion one of the best available of Ford Island, the USS *Arizona* Memorial and surrounding sections of Oʻahu, stretching out past the Pearl City Peninsula.

Wrap around the observation deck and head downstairs (green arrows point the way) to the navigation bridge on level 04. This close-quartered area was used for daily navigation and wartime operations. Outdated navigational equipment can still be found here, making this a fun make-believe area for the young and young at heart. Just around the corner you will find the original chart room and command office.

BELOW DECKS

To enter the lower decks of the USS *Missouri*, head to the stern of the ship on the main deck level and look for the "doghouse" entrance to the hatch and stairwell. This "doghouse," is the central cube-shaped Aviation compartment immediately adjacent to the down-hatch providing access below decks.

Descending down the ladders, you will land in one of two connected enlisted mess decks, a once bustling center of the ship where thousands of meals were served a day to the 3,000-man crew. Following the tour arrows, you head out of the "Teakwood Inn" mess hall on the first half of your below-decks tour.

The Crew's Room

The Crew's Room is a collection of artifacts donated by former crewmembers of all ranks and period, reflecting their memories of service aboard the USS *Missouri*, from her commissioning through each overseas battle up to her final retirement. This miniature museum-within-a-museum is worth a stop.

The Chief Petty Officer's Legacy Center

Chief petty officers were the hands-on leaders of the enlisted men and managers of the ship's departments. Charged with being role models for younger enlisted men, CPO's by the end of day had been on duty long enough to deserve a little break separate here from the enlisted men to talk over the ship's business

These sleeping quarters, two to a room, were the roomier version had by younger officers and chiefs. Most sailors slept in open bunks with little to no privacy.

with their colleagues. The legacy center has a small museum describing the life of a navy chief onboard the USS *Missouri*, continuing with a tour of their lounge area and separate dining quarters. Eighty-two chiefs would have served at a time on the Mighty Mo, including boatswain's chiefs, gunnersmate chiefs, and engineering chiefs, to name a few.

Included in the legacy area is the ship's library, which can be viewed through a half-door opening. Notice that this is not your average silent reading space, but instead a humming, belly-of-the-ship room. Still, it was a refuge for those who needed to write a letter, escape in a good read, or teach themselves through books written on any number of topics.

Wrapping around past your first view of the galley, you will reenter the Teakwood Inn mess hall and head straight out, moving in the opposite direction of the hall.

Truman Line

Imagine lining up for your daily meal, sweaty from a day's work on deck, and next to you in line is none other than Margaret Truman, daughter of then President Harry S. Truman. In honor of Margaret and her famous father, the mess deck below decks became fondly known as the Truman Line.

Here you will also see the galley office where occurred the massive undertaking of ordering food supplies. Imagine if you will, buying milk for your family, and then imagine buying milk for 3,000 men. This was no small task and kept the food service personnel working 'round the clock to supply the USS *Missouri*'s many galleys and mess halls.

The Bakeries

Feeding a crew the size of a small town requires a mighty force of bakers and chefs. From the Mighty Mo's bakeshops each day came hundreds of pies, loaves of bread, and other tasty baked goods. You can almost smell the warm dough rising as you pass by these tight-quartered but well-equipped kitchens.

Further Below Decks Exploring

Beyond the bakeries is a new exhibit showcasing World War II photos. You make a U-turn at the end of this exhibit and head back past the bakeries and master at arms office. Then move on to the marine quarters, the machine shop, showers, supplies office, "coffin-rack" bunks for hundreds of enlisted men, command master chief office, ship's newsletter office, weapons office, engineering department, lawyer, state rooms for warrant officers, computer center and classroom, dental lab, ammunition hoist, and post office. Leaving below decks you will exit into the ward room and officers mess.

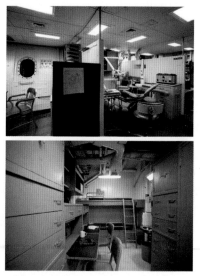

Life on board the USS Missouri *included regular dental care and medical visits.*

4

Pacific Aviation Museum Pearl Harbor

Chances are, if you've dreamed of piloting a MiG fighter jet, navigating a canvas-winged Stinson airplane, or of saving hundreds of lives from the decks of a Sikorsky SH-3 Sea King helicopter, the Pacific Aviation Museum Pearl Harbor will be some sort of fantasyland for you. Opened in 2006, the Pacific Aviation Museum Pearl Harbor is TripAdvisor.com's #8 aviation attraction, and for good reason. From the Curtiss P-40E Warhawk fighter, to the B-25B Mitchell bomber, the Aviation Museum's collection is alive and growing.

The Ford Island Field Control Tower can be seen from several locations around O'ahu. It greets visitors at the entrance to the Pacific Aviation Museum.

Housed in historic hangars 37 and 79 adjacent to Ford Island's Luke Airfield, the Aviation Museum is staffed by a crew of dedicated volunteers and docents expert in knowledge of Pacific aviation history. Hangar 79 looks much as did in 1941 and still bares witness to the attack on Pearl Harbor, with bullet-riddled windows set high in its hangar doors. Visitors walk

Hangar 79 at Ford Island's Pacific Aviation Museum Pearl Harbor has a rotating display of planes large and small and a working restoration shop for visitors to see. The Pacific Aviation Museum Pearl Harbor has future plans for this hangar, including two floors of interactive exhibits.

through the aviation history of the Pacific in both hangars, not the least of which chapter is the December 7 attacks on Pearl Harbor. The prominent orange and white control tower at the gates to this impressive collection of aviation history stands watch over Ford Island, was refurbished in 2011, and is scheduled to soon welcome visitors.

For the aviation aficionado, Hangars 37 and 79 take a good two hours to navigate through. Younger visitors might swoop through the exhibits a bit more quickly, and real experts could spend the good part of a day reveling in the winged exhibits.

Ford Island's airfields and hangars are home to ties to the life of celebrity flyers, such as Amelia Earhart's ground-loop in 1937 and a display of the actual Stearman N2S-3 in which former President George H.W. Bush learned to fly while serving in the navy during World War II.

No small stop on your tour of the Pearl Harbor historic sites, the Pacific Aviation Museum Pearl Harbor will undoubtedly please visitors of all ages.

HANGAR 37

» Murals

Make sure to look up and down when you tour this hangar, as great thought has been put into each detail. The floor mural laid out at the front atrium offers a bird's-eye view of O'ahu, with Ford Island and the surrounding Pearl City-Aiea area shown near the ticket booth and gift store. Inside Hangar 37 you encounter several more floor and wall murals that recount aviation history in the Pacific.

Hangar 37 at the Pacific Aviation Museum Pearl Harbor includes several murals depicting O'ahu and the Pacific during WWII.

» Gallery and Theater

The Pacific Aviation Museum theater daily plays a historical film detailing the importance of aviation in the Pacific during World War II. Outside the theater doors you find small displays dedicated to Pan Am and the pioneer airline's early China Clipper Ship flights to Hawai'i.

» Ford Island Mural and *Kaga* Model Aircraft Carrier

Rounding the Hawaiian tunnel and into the main hangar space, you will notice a wall mural depicting Ford Island as it looked just before the Pearl Harbor attacks. If you've already visited the USS *Arizona* Memorial, then this map will help guide you in connecting the planes in this exhibit to the Pearl Harbor attack. If you're just beginning your exploration of Ford Island and Pearl Harbor, then take note of the map and of ships around the perimeter of Battleship Row. It was the placement of vessels and planes that day, December 7, 1941, that made them easy targets when the Japanese Imperial Forces arrived.

Here you will also find a model on display of the *Kaga* aircraft carrier, a replica of the ship that carried dozens of Japanese warplanes silently across the Pacific to take part in the surprise attack on the American Forces that fateful day in 1941.

A mural just inside Hangar 37 describes the scene at Ford Island as the first Japanese fighter pilots swooped in for attack on December 7, 1941.

» Mitsubishi A6M2 Model 21 Type 0 – "Zero" (Naval Carrier-based Fighter)

The Zero (referred to by American servicemen as a Zeke) was considered for much of World War II to be one of the best fighting planes in production. To the Allied forces' surprise, it could outmaneuver and outrange their fighter planes. However, the Zero's light construction made it weak when hit by bullets, causing its eventual downfall. When you tour the USS *Missouri* you will most likely visit the Kamikaze Deck, on her starboard side. There, on April 11, 1945, a Japanese "Zeke" hurled itself kamikaze-style at the USS *Missouri* in hopes of causing casualties. This suicide bomber's pilot was eventually found in the rubble and given an honorable burial at sea by the USS *Missouri's* captain and crew. It can be hard to respect the enemy in times of war, but in this case, what Captain Callaghan saw was a young man fighting for his country, just as all of his crew did for theirs.

The Zero on display is one of the six remaining original Mitsubishi A6M2 Zeros worldwide. The fighter was downed

A Japanese "Zero" in mock flight preparation at Hangar 37.

in a jungle during the battle in the Solomon Islands, not to be recovered until 1964, and it was restored to flying status in the 1980s.

The Niʻihau Zero Incident

As the Japanese forces made their second wave attack on Pearl Harbor, December 7, one Zero Mitsubishi A6M2, hit by anti-aircraft fire from the ground, crash-landed on Niʻihau, the small island located west of Kauaʻi. Pilot Shigenori Nishikaichi survived the landing, was aided by a local Japanese resident, and took hostage other island residents. Niʻihauan Ben Kanehele and his wife would have none of it, though, and overpowered Nishikaichi, killing him. The plane crashed by Nishikaichi, a famed Japanese Zero, was recovered and picked over by the U.S. government in an attempt to understand the workings of this amazing aircraft.

A Rare Find

Parts taken from the Zero from the Niʻihau Incident are on display

Visitors can view the skeletal frame of a "Zero" that crash-landed.

at the Pacific Aviation Museum and are being shown to the public for the first time.

» North American B-25B Mitchell (Medium Bomber)

This display of a B-25B bomber was assembled from parts salvaged from many B-25Bs. Few of these workhorse World War II bombers survive today. During the early war years, B-25Bs were only lightly armed, but by the end of the war the Mitchell bomber would be one of the most heavily armored attack planes.

» The Doolittle Raid

What America needed after the Pearl Harbor attack losses and ensuing defeats in the Pacific was a morale boost. In response, the Army Air Corp's Lt. Col. Jimmy Doolittle hatched a plan that seemed so outrageous few could imagine its success. Doolittle decided to use sixteen land-based B-25 bombers launched

A restored B-25 Bomber, like those used in the Doolittle Raid, is on display in Hangar 37.

An Army Air Force B-25B bomber takes off from USS Hornet *(CV-8) at the start of the raid, 18 April 1942. Note men watching from the signal lamp platform at right.*

precariously from the deck of an aircraft carrier to deliver a direct surprise hit on Japan. In April 1942, 200 miles before reaching the location of their carefully-planned launch site, due to being spotted by a Japanese ship, the Doolittle Raid commenced. Because of flying the extra miles, all sixteen bombers were forced to crash land when they prematurely ran out of fuel. Despite this, seventy-three of the eighty crewmen survived, picked up off and along the coasts of Japan, China and Russia.

» Battle of Midway Display and the Douglas SBD Dauntless (Dive Bomber)

The Battle of Midway marked a turning point in the Pacific during World War II when the U.S. regained their naval strength over Japan. Perhaps it was just luck, but Midway turned the tide for the Allied forces, and the Japanese military's downward spiral began. Four of the six Japanese aircraft carriers used in the Pearl Harbor attacks were taken out near Midway Atoll in a stunning victory for the U.S. Navy.

The pilots flying a SBD Dauntless played a crucial role in the

Battle of Midway, sinking all four Japanese aircraft carriers. Considered obsolete by World War II, the Dauntless came back with a vengeance, proving to be a "slow, but deadly" force against the enemy.

» The F4F-3 Wildcat

The Wildcat on display at the Pacific Aviation Museum was accepted into navy service in 1943.

Not every plane arrives at the Pacific Aviation Museum in tip-top shape. Here a SBD Dauntless with considerable corrosion enters the shop for repairs and restoration.

Her pilot ditched her over the chilly waters of Lake Michigan due to a tragic mechanical failure, just three months into service. The Wildcat sank in 220 feet of water to the bed of Lake Michigan. She sat there, preserved by cool freshwater, until 1991 when she was recovered in near-perfect condition. Unlike later Wildcat builds, designed for use on tightly spaced aircraft carrier decks, this plane lacks foldable wings.

During the Guadalcanal campaign in 1943, U.S. forces took real estate from Japan for the first time in World War II. The Wildcats gave pilots strong firepower and the ability to employ superior tactics in the air. Despite these attributes,

Hangar 37 at the Pacific Aviation Museum Pearl Harbor houses more permanent displays, with engaging models alongside them. Seen here is an F4F-3 Wildcat, recovered in 1990 from a muddy lake bottom and restored to its former glory for display.

the Wildcats were known to be demanding on pilots and untrustworthy when landing.

» Amelia Earhart Theater

Make sure to stop into the small but interesting Amelia Earhart Theater. Lining the walls are photographs of the aviator's time in Hawai'i and historical facts about her pioneering aviation flights.

» Boeing N2S-3 Stearman (Trainer)

Amelia and Dorothy Leslie arrive in 1934.

This Stearman was flown by none other than President George Herbert Walker Bush during his primary flight training in 1942. The young President Bush, then 18 years old, signed up for the service along with thousands of other young men from across the nation, ready to defend their coun-

Amelia and Duke Kahanamoku, 1935.

try. This cheerful-looking yellow Stearman went on to a hard-working post-war life as a crop duster, used until 1987 when she was put in storage following a crash.

» Aeronca Model 65TC

The Aeronca TC-65 Defender was an American high-wing light plane of the 1940s. The beginning of World War II ushered in a new era for Aeronca aircraft. Production of the TC-65 Defender was increased when the U.S. government decided to

This Aeronica TC-65 was one of just a few civilian planes in the air on the morning of December 7, 1941.

use the plane for its new Civilian Pilot Training (CPT) program, created to train new pilots for wartime service.

Eight privately owned airplanes were in the air over Oʻahu at time of the December 7 attacks on Pearl Harbor. Roy Vitousek and his son Martin were flying this Defender toward Pearl Harbor when the Japanese began firing. According to Martin, they stayed in the air during part of the attack, circling at 2,000 feet to avoid the Japanese planes. Upon taking enemy fire, they returned to the Territory of Hawaiʻi's John Rodgers Field for a safe landing. John Rodgers Field, greatly increased in size and capabilities after World War II, became Honolulu International Airport.

» Curtiss P-40E Warhawk (Pursuit Fighter)

See Hangar 79 section (pg 68-69) for more information.

HANGAR 79

» Lt. Ted Shealy's Restoration Shop

The creation of this aircraft restoration shop was proposed to the museum in 2007 by Mike and Carol Shealy, relatives of navy man Ted Shealy. Ted Shealy served aboard the USS *Enterprise* at Pearl Harbor and then again at Air Station Barber's Point in the 1940s serving as chief warrant officer in charge of the Assembly and Repair Department. Today, the Ted Shealy Restoration Shop is an active, buzzing aviation mechanics wonderland. Visitors are likely to be taken under the wings by one of the many volunteer docents and shown the ins-and-outs of aviation repair.

Not to be missed is the Aviator's Tour, a behind-the-scenes look at our Hangar 79 Restoration Shop. You'll see aircraft such as the F-15 Eagle and the F-14 Tomcat and learn about aircraft manufacturing.

Volunteers lovingly restore aircraft in the Lt. Ted Shealy Restoration Shop.

Hangar 79 houses two Russian-made MiG fighter jets alongside its many helicopter models.

» The Planes and Helicopters of the Pacific Aviation Museum

The collection at the Pacific Aviation Museum Pearl Harbor grows by the year. Thanks to generous worldwide donations, curators have worked diligently to create a diverse and intriguing collection of aircraft. From the impeccably restored Japanese Zero (Mitsubishi A6M2) housed in Hangar 37 to the up-and-coming restoration of a B-17 recovered from the swamps of new Guinea, there is a slice of aviation history for everyone.

Some of the planes and helicopters are found parked outside of Hangar 79, on the surrounding grounds, and some are housed inside the hangar. The displays are moved as needed to accommodate new arrivals and new restoration work; if you're unable to find a particular plane, ask a docent to guide you.

» Hangar 79 Doors

As you enter Hangar 79, take a moment to stop and turn around, gazing upwards to the blue wire-filled window pains. Notice they are riddled with bullet holes. Japanese fighter planes shot out these holes on December 7, 1941, as they made pass after pass over Ford Island. No matter how great the improvements to Ford Island and Pearl Harbor, and even amidst the beauty of the Pacific Aviation Museum's lovingly restored aircraft, these bullet holes remain as a solemn reminder of the fear and destruction that spread that day on O'ahu. If you're having trouble spotting the windows, don't hesitate to ask a docent for help.

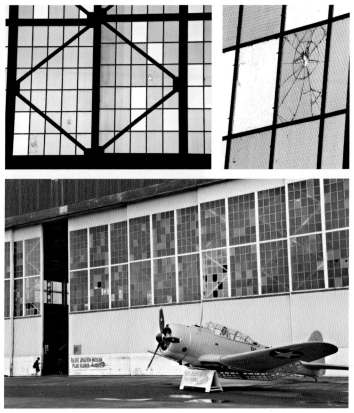

Bullet holes still mark the windows of Hangar 79.

» The China Burma India Theater
   – 14th Air Service Group

When it became clear that Japan had taken out Pearl Harbor with the intent of conquering the Pacific and Asia, a first-line-of-defense goal for the United States was to help secure nations next on Japan's hit list, including China and her neighboring countries. One hundred Curtiss P-40 Warhawks, originally slated for service in defending England against the German Luftwaffe, were redirected to Kunming, China, to the 14th Air Service Group, the famed "Flying Tigers," under the leadership of Major General Claire Lee Chennault. Chennault would until 1945 lead with incredible success these volunteer pilots and ground forces.

Curtiss P-40 Warhawk

While the Japanese had the Zero, the Americans had the Warhawk, a slower but tougher aerial war machine. Over 14,000 Warhawks were built during World War II, flown by militaries of nations all over the world. "The Flying Ti-

A Curtiss P-40 Warhawk gets a little sun.

gers" is just one configuration of the Curtiss P-40 to make their mark on the aviation world. Flying Tiger pilots are credited with 299 confirmed enemy aircraft destroyed during their service in 1941-1942. The fighter featured here in Hangar 79 flew primarily as a trainer for the Royal Air Force in Great Britain. It changed ownership before being shipped to Hawai'i in 1969 for the filming of the big-budget Pearl Harbor attack movie, *Tora! Tora! Tora!*

The Pacific Aviation Museum's P-40 Warhawk is an excellent example of the West's rugged answer to the lightweight Japanese "Zero."

» Northrop Freedom Fighter F-5A/T-38

The F-5A on display at Pacific Aviation Museum is one of four acquired by the Imperial Iranian Air Force in 1969. It was likely based at Chan Bahar Air Base and charged with the defense of the Strait of Hormuz. Transferred to Jordan in 1974, this F-5A

later returned to the United States. The aircraft is painted in Republic of Korea Air Force markings, circa 1965. Korea was one of the first buyers of the F-5A, which were involved in several border incidents – most details of which remain classified. This particular aircraft honors Gen. Kim Too Man, a legendary figure in the Republic of Korea Air Force (ROKAF).

» General Dynamics F-111C Aardvark (Fighter-bomber)

Designed as a fighter jet, the Aardvark was used instead for tactical bombing, able to drop an 8,000-pound bomb on target, up to 1,500 miles away. The F-111C pioneered several technologies for production aircraft, including variable-sweep wings, afterburning turbofan engines, and automated terrain-following radar for low-level, high-speed flight. This jet was restored and presented in 2013 to the Pacific Aviation Museum by the Royal Australian Air Force.

» MiG

The MiG (short for manufacturer Mikoyan-Gurevich) was developed by the Soviet Union following World War II. The MiG series of planes would become known worldwide for their engineering and used in battle by the Soviet Union and its allies, including

North Vietnam, during the Vietnam War. The Pacific Aviation Museum is home to two models, the MiG-15 and MiG-21.

» Additional airplanes housed in hangar 79

F-86 Sabre "Nina"
F-102 Delta Dagger
McDonnell Douglas F-15A "Eagle"
F-14 "Tomcat"
Lockheed F-104A "Starfighter"
Lockheed T-33 "Shooting Star"
F-4 Phantom
T-6 Texan
B-52 Nose Section
B-17 E Flying Fortress

Lockheed F-104A "Starfighter"

» Helicopters in Hangar 79

CH-34 Choctaw
UH-1 Iroquois "Huey"
Bell AH-1S "Cobra"
Sikorsky SH-60B "Seahawk"
Sikorsky SH-3H "Sea King"
Sikorsky CH-53 D "Sea Stallion"

Sikorsky SH-3H "Sea King"

AMELIA EARHART IN HAWAI'I

Amelia Earhart first visited Hawai'i in December 1934, arriving by ship with her plane, a Lockheed Vega. She embarked on her record-breaking flight from the Army Air Corp's Wheeler Field in Central O'ahu to Oakland, California, on January 11, 1935, becoming the first person to fly solo across the Pacific. In March 1937, Earhart returned to Hawai'i to fly the first leg of what would become her fateful attempted westbound around-the-world flight. Her flight plan was sidelined temporarily when a flat tire during takeoff on Ford Island caused damage to her custom-built Electra airplane. She eventually again tried this fight in her attempt to circumnavigate

Amelia with Army weather experts. She had just arrived at Wheeler Field from Oakland on her Lockheed Electra for her round-the-world flight.

Amelia back again in Hawai'i for her round-the-world flight (March 18-20, 1937). Amelia ground looped her plane, damaging the tire and making it unable to fly.

the globe, this time eastbound, but of course, her fate is well known. She would lose radio contact in June of 1937, near the equator southwest of Hawai'i, disappearing forever on her way around the world.

THE TOWER

The Ford Island Field Control Tower is the 158-foot tall, orange and white (and hard to miss), recently restored landmark that stands outside of Hangar 37. The tower was under construction during the attacks in 1941, but its control center at its base had been completed and was where this now famous radio call went out: "AIR RAID PEARL HARBOR THIS IS NO DRILL."

Before (left), and after restoration of the Ford Island Field Control Tower.

A frequent misconception is that this tower was used for submariners training, but in fact, a similar tower across the West Loch of Pearl Harbor is where those deepwater trainings would have occurred. Today the tower is visible from many areas of O'ahu, a beacon to the Ford Island historic sites.

5

The USS *Bowfin* Submarine Museum and Park

USS *BOWFIN* SUBMARINE (SS-287) THE "PEARL HARBOR AVENGER"

Balao-Class Submarine–Launched December 7, 1942 Kittery, Maine

It took a strong constitution to survive life aboard a submarine for months on end. Living inside a 16-foot diameter tube, submerged below hundreds of feet of seawater is hard enough alone, but imagine doing it with 80 other men while navigating waters peppered with depth charges.

Despite the grueling conditions, the USS *Bowfin* and her crews sank a record number of ships in her short sea service. The USS *Bowfin* sank roughly 23 vessels (though the actual number is widely contested and could be as high as 44), accounting for one of the highest "kill rates" of an American sub in World War II. This Balao-class vessel was built for stealth, with a stronger pressure hull achieved through welding, instead of riveting, allowing her to submerge a full 100 feet deeper than earlier submarine classes.

Commissioned one year after the attacks on December 7, 1942, the USS *Bowfin* became aptly nicknamed "The Pearl Harbor Avenger." And avenge she would. Four captains in

The USS Bowfin *Submarine, docked permanently at the WWII Valor in the Pacific National Monument.*

four years would lead her through enemy waters time and time again back to safety. The USS *Bowfin* returned from mothball storage to the waters of Pearl Harbor in 1981 to become the centerpiece of a permanent submarine museum. Today thousands of visitors take a dive below decks to reimagine life aboard a World War II-era submarine.

All visitors to the USS *Bowfin* Submarine and Museum receive a complimentary audio tour to take along while exploring. This is a well-narrated, self-paced audio tour with lots of information. There is a child-friendly (or short attention span) version, which the docents can help you access.

Statistics

Length: Exterior tube 311.6 ft., interior tube 289 ft.
Diameter: 27.3 ft. (16 ft. diameter interior tube)
Displacement: 1,525 tons—small in comparison to other subs
Crew: 80 men, 10 officers, 70 enlisted

The Layout

The USS *Bowfin* is sectioned into eight interior compartments for easy containment in case of battle damage. Following the audio tour, you are guided through each section, provided with ample information on life below decks.

» **Here is a a list of each area found within the living and operating quarters of the USS *Bowfin*.**

Forward Torpedo Room

The forward torpedo room is the first area visitors enter; the sub has ten torpedo tubes in total and could carry a total of twenty-four torpedoes.

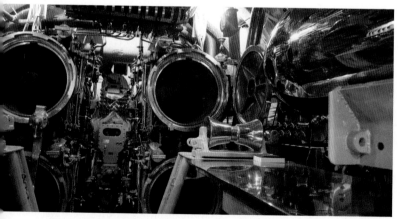

Torpedo tubes are deceptively beautiful at the fore and aft of the vessel.

Yeoman's Office

The yeoman's office handled all administrative issues on the ship, including personnel records and pay.

Captain's Cabin

Sleeping quarters with this much room could only be reserved for the captain of the ship. He would have used the indicators overhead in his bunk to track the USS *Bowfin's* depth and course at all hours of the day and night.

Visitors navigate the narrow bunk area, which also serves as a hallway, aboard the USS Bowfin.

Control Room

Air manifold controls, diving controls, and radar displays were all housed here, aiding in the general maneuvering of this large vessel.

A dizzying array of control panels and measurement devices deck the walls of the control room and other areas of the USS Bowfin.

Twin Periscopes

The twin periscopes were used by the captain to command the ship during submerged attacks. At full extension the USS *Bowfin's* periscopes reached six stories high, allowing the captain a view above water when safely hidden far below the sea.

A visitor on shore peers into a periscope.

Radio Room

This was the communication center of the ship, keeping USS *Bowfin* and her crew up to date on the world around her with command instructions and vital task information.

Kitchen and Mess Hall

It was claimed that the submarine fleet of the U.S. Navy had some of the best cooks around. We know they must have been the most organized on the USS *Bowfin*, because cooking space was slim and had to require a dance of culinary expertise in preparing meals for eighty sailors. Meals were eaten in shifts, with sailors waiting for a turn in the small dining area. Much like the sleeping quarters, the dining room could only accommodate some of the crew. Despite the tight quarters, cooks managed to produce foods fit for kings that no doubt were a welcome break to the sometimes-monotonous days spent underwater.

Bunks

Sailors slept in shifts, sharing beds much as they shared dining room chairs, plates, and time in the small restroom. This practice was called "hot-bunking."

Crew members slept in shifts aboard the USS Bowfin. *"Hot-bunking" was commonplace on submarines, maximizing space.*

Twin-Engine Rooms

The USS *Bowfin* has four 16-cylinder diesel engines powering four GE generators. These generators charge batteries which power two 8-foot propellers that could drive the submarine on the surface at 20 knots, or nearly 25 MPH. The USS *Bowfin* carried enough fuel to keep her patrolling for three months.

Maneuvering Room

This area of the ship delights visitors young and old today with its impressive array of knobs and levers. Imagine for a moment steering a vessel like the USS *Bowfin* through an underwater labyrinth of mines, using navigation equipment and intuition from the darkened interior of the ship.

Second Torpedo Room

Rounding out your USS *Bowfin* below decks tour is the aft torpedo room. Watch your step heading to the after deck above you.

After Deck

The after deck (everything above water) includes a look at three topside guns, one 5-inch 25-caliber (Mk 40), one 40-millimeter (Mk 3) and one 20-millimeter (Mk 10).

The "Don't Tread on Me" jack flag, one of the earliest flags used by the U.S. Navy, flies above the USS *Bowfin*.

"Don't Tread on Me" is flown above the after deck of the USS Bowfin.

USS *Bowfin* Submarine Museum and Park

Adjacent to the entrance to the USS *Bowfin* Submarine is the USS *Bowfin* Museum, which holds a collection of over 4,000 artifacts relating to submariners in the Pacific and the history of the submarine and the U.S. Navy. We highly recommend this stop as another natural place to unwind during your tour day, out of the sun and heat. Walking this 10,000-square-foot facility is also a welcome relief to those who suffered from claustrophobia on their submarine tour. The museum is accompanied by its own audio tour.

Memorial Park

Between the USS *Bowfin* Submarine and the World War II Valor in the Pacific Monuments, guests find a waterfront memorial to the 3,500 submariners lost at sea during World War II and their fifty-two submarines. Walking this semicircle fronting the waters of Pearl Harbor is a time for somber remembrance of those who embraced this dangerous underwater navy duty.

The grounds of the USS Bowfin *Museum*

The grounds of the USS Bowfin *Museum*

SIX

The USS *Arizona* Memorial and World War II Valor in the Pacific National Monument

S aturday, December 6, 1941: Darkness has settled over Pearl Harbor on Oʻahu's south shore. Thousands of sailors, Marines, and soldiers are returning from leave, working their duty stations, or sleeping off a weekend of fun. It is unimaginable to think that just a few hundred miles north of Oʻahu, dozens of Japanese bomber carrier planes were being made ready for a stealthy attack flight to the Hawaiian Islands.

The attack by Japanese Imperial forces was well planned, with planes entering from the north. The first wave swooped down over Pearl Harbor and Ford Island shortly after dawn on Sunday, December 7, 1941, creating havoc and changing history forever.

At 8:06 AM, a 1,760-pound, armor-piercing bomb hit the USS *Arizona's* forward deck, detonating an ammunition magazine, creating an explosion seen and heard miles away. The USS *Arizona* sank within minutes in Battleship Row along the east shore of Ford Island, chaos raining down around her.

Caught by surprise and unprepared, the men working the docks and on board the many battleships and cruisers moored up near Battleship Row fell victim to the ruthless sneak attack. Survivors watched in shock and horror, seeing ships exploding,

The USS Arizona sinking in the waters of Pearl Harbor on December 7, 1941

buildings catching on fire, oil burning in the water around the ships injuring and killing those who managed to jump to safety. The scene was total havoc.

By the second wave of attacks, some sailors and soldiers managed to man their guns, ready to fire back at the attacking planes. The Japanese would be less successful in this attempt, begun 30 minutes after the first wave pilots headed back to their carriers. By 9:55 AM, the Pearl Harbor base was heavily damaged and four battleships were sunk.

What the Japanese armed forces probably didn't count on that day was the incredible resolve of the people of Hawai'i and mainland America. Almost every battleship sunk was resurrected and returned to duty within the next few years. The USS *Arizona*, with 900 men entombed in its sunken hull, lost 1,177 altogether. She was left where she lay, a memorial to her fallen

The USS Arizona Memorial as seen from the water. The Tree of Life is represented in the smaller windows to the far right.

An aerial views that most visitors won't see illustrates the massive structure of the USS Arizona sunk below Pearl Harbor's waters.

crew. The USS *Utah* and USS *Oklahoma* battleships were also too badly damaged to save. The USS *Utah*, too, became a living tomb for her sailors.

A memorial was erected in 1962 alongside the USS *Arizona's* submerged hull (the superstructure was removed after World War II) thanks to a fundraising campaign run from 1958 through 1961. The cost was around $400,000 and paid for with funding from the Territory of Hawai'i, donations made by individuals including from an Elvis Presley concert at Pearl Harbor's Bloch Arena, the sale of plastic models of the USS *Arizona*, and through funds appropriated by Congress.

Honolulu architect Alfred Preis designed the memorial, creating an arched, white-stone design meant to represent the height of America before the war, our dip into sadness and grief during the attacks on Pearl Harbor, and then our resurrection and rebirth as a stronger nation. The Tree of Life is represented in the twenty-one windows that open out from the memorial's Shrine room, a feature seen easily from onshore.

» Theater Briefing

All ticket holders to the USS *Arizona* Memorial are required to watch a twenty-three-minute briefing video narrated by Stockard Channing. You will not regret this time spent reflecting on the moments aboard the USS *Arizona* before, during, and after the Pearl Harbor attacks. After the film, park rangers escort you to a nearby waiting shuttle boat moored outside of the theater. The boats carry visitors to the USS *Arizona* in fifteen-minute intervals.

» For Your Safety

All visitors should remain seated during the boat ride. Please don't stand up onboard the launch to take photos; photo opportunities will be available once on the memorial.

» On Board the USS *Arizona* Memorial

While visiting the sunken hull of the USS *Arizona*, be sure to walk the entire length of the structure. On entering you will notice tall white rooms, a sign of peace and tranquility floating above the waters of Pearl Harbor. In the sagging center area of

At the center of USS Arizona *Memorial is a map detailing the direction in relation to the memorial and the size of the sunken hull.*

the memorial, which represents the attacks on Pearl Harbor and the great losses suffered in World War II, you will find a map detailing the direction in relation to the memorial and size of the USS *Arizona* hull. A large viewing hole allows visitors to peer down into the water near the shrine-end of the memorial. There fish swim about the water, and sea life reclaims the rusting metal of USS *Arizona's* decks.

Visitors gaze into the waters above the USS Arizona *from the memorial decks.*

At the far end of the memorial, the Shrine Room is a somber setting that often elicits prayer and calm from visitors as they read the 1,177 names of sailors and Marines who lost their lives. Leis are often left in memory of loved ones, a fresh reminder of this not-so-long-ago wound.

Stop halfway across the memorial on your way out and look towards the USS *Missouri*. You may find an oil sheen on the water's surface here. This oil, which bubbles up periodically, has been escaping the hull of the USS *Arizona* now for over seventy years. It is a ghastly reminder of how recent the Pearl Harbor attack was, how real it still is today.

» Alfred Preis

In a poetic gesture, the man chosen to design the USS *Arizona* Memorial was himself an escapee from the Nazis of Austria in the 1930s. Refugee Alfred Preis landed in Honolulu after the attacks at Pearl Harbor only to be placed in an internment camp at Sand Island due to his connections to Germany. Of course, he was also a victim of World War II; his contribution to the design of the USS *Arizona* Memorial is a good example of the healing provided to many by this historic site.

Onboard the USS Arizona *Memorial, visitors observe the wall of names in the Shrine Room.*

» The Visitor Center Museums and Grounds

The World War II Valor in the Pacific National Monument features two museums on-site. They face each other near the entrance to the USS *Arizona* Memorial Theater. Each museum presents a decidedly different tone, while both are connected throughout by the thread of human existence in the face of war in Hawai'i and the Pacific.

Leave at least 30 minutes in your schedule to spend time walking through the two museums, either before or after your tour of the USS *Arizona* Memorial.

The tour begins at the "Road to War" museum. There visitors listening to the audio tour hear the actual voices of survivors retelling their stories of the Pearl Harbor attacks and post-war Hawai'i. View decoding machines, models of the battleship USS *Arizona* and the Japanese aircraft carrier IMS *Akagi,* which led the attack on Pearl Harbor, and reflect on the last-ditch effort by President Franklin Delano Roosevelt to halt

Japan's advances in the Pacific prior to the Pearl Harbor attacks.

Across the court is the "Attack Gallery," presenting a somber look at the what-ifs of December 7, 1941. The Opana Incident highlights how newly installed radar gave ample warning of a pending attack to the island of O'ahu and its military bases, but it was in fact so new that few were trained to read it correctly. No one could have guessed what those blips on the radar screen really meant. In addition, this gallery showcases photographs taken just after the attacks that horrifically portray the death and destruction.

» USS *Arizona* Anchor

Not to be missed on your tour of the grounds at the Pearl Harbor Visitor Center is one of the anchors from the USS *Arizona*. Salvaged 200 feet away from where the ship sunk, this

A Japanese Zero prepares to launch from an aircraft carrier in the Pacific.

19,000-pound relic is no small piece of iron. Standing below the anchor is a poignant reminder of the battleship USS *Arizona's* sheer size and of the emotional weight of this attack on Hawai'i and America as a nation. The United States and its Allies would go on to win World War II, but not before many lives were sacrificed in the fight, beginning with those lost here at Pearl Harbor.

» The USS *Arizona* (BB-39)

The USS *Arizona* was a Pennsylvania-class battleship commissioned in 1916 in honor of the forty-eighth state admitted to the Union. A super-dreadnought battleship, she escorted

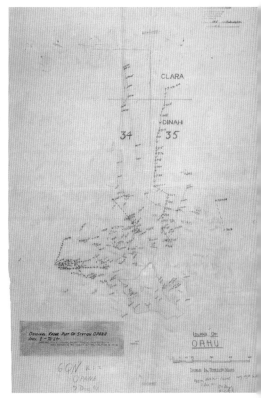

A copy of the radar plot from detector station Opana shows the path of Japanese planes arriving in Hawai'i December 7, 1941.

President Woodrow Wilson to the Paris Peace Conference in 1919, then departed, sent to Turkey during the Greco-Turkish war. Eventually the USS *Arizona* made her way, after some modernization, to the Pacific Fleet, where she would unexpectedly remain forever.

"Let our grief for the men of the USS *Arizona* be for all those whose futures were taken from them December Seventh 1941. Here they will never be forgotten."
—Stockard Channing, *Death of the* Arizona

» The USS *Arizona* Band

Nearly half of the casualties from the Pearl Harbor attacks occurred on the battleship USS *Arizona*. Among the 1,177 crewmen killed were all twenty-one members of the USS *Arizona's* band, known as U.S. Navy Band Unit (NBU) 22, who when the attack began were on deck preparing to play music for the ship's daily flag-raising ceremony. This is the only time in American military history that an entire military band was killed in action.

» Families in Mourning

There were thirty-seven sets (some were trios) of brothers assigned to the USS *Arizona* on December 7, 1941. Of these thirty-seven families represented, twenty-three pairs of brothers died during the attack. Only one pair of brothers, Kenneth and Russell Warriner, both survived the attack: Kenneth was away at flight school and Russell was injured but recovered. The ship's only father-and-son pair, Thomas Augusta Free and his son William Thomas Free, were both killed in action that day.

7

Beyond Pearl Harbor and Ford Island– Significant Military Sites of O'ahu

PUNCHBOWL CEMETERY

Above the downtown area of Honolulu, Punchbowl Cemetery, once known as Pūowaina, or "Hill of Sacrifice", is today home to the National Memorial Cemetery of the Pacific. Over 53,000 who served or were related to those who fought in World Wars I & II, and the Korean and Vietnam wars are laid to rest here. The "Courts of the Missing", an elegant stone and marble monument found at the far end of the cemetery grounds, memorialize the 26,280 servicemen listed missing in action in the Pacific, and is a dramatic focal point of the cemetery. Including such notables as famed war reporter Ernie Pyle, and the late Senator and Medal of Honor recipient Daniel K. Inouye. Visitors can walk along a memorial pathway that is lined with a variety of memorials

Punchbowl Cemetery is both solemn and beautiful.

that honor America's veterans from various branches of the U.S. military, most commemorating soldiers of our 20th-century wars, including those killed at Pearl Harbor.

This large and lush crater was created when lava and steam erupted from the coral beds below the Koʻolau mountains over 75,000 years ago. Its beauty is grand, and the seclusion the crater walls provide give this scared place a tranquil feel. A visit here is a memorable end to a day of exploring the Pearl Harbor and Ford Island military sites, helping to tell the whole story of life, and the military, in the Pacific theater.

Punchbowl Cemetery is open daily.

September 30 – March 1: 8:00 AM to 5:30 PM
March 2 – September 29: 8:00 AM to 6:30 PM
On Memorial Day, the cemetery is open from 7:00 AM until 7:00 PM

Getting there:

2177 Puowaina Dr, Honolulu, HI 96813 (808) 532-3720

FORT DERUSSY

While strolling along the beach walks of Waikīkī, you may encounter a somewhat out-of-place military site: Fort DeRussy. An army relic, Fort DeRussy speaks to a time gone by when protecting Oʻahu meant mil-

The entrance to Fort DeRussy is nestled amid hotels and beach front in busy Waikīkī.

itary installations at every turn. The Fort DeRussy Museum is housed in Battery Randolph, a reinforced concrete emplacement with roofs as much as 12 feet thick. The battery was built around 1911 to hold two 14-inch guns that could fire projectiles as far as 14 miles. Battery Randolph protected Honolulu Harbor from invasion as part of a coastal defense system. Were it not a defensive military structure it might not have survived the development of Waikīkī. Today visitors can meander in for a friendly look at the U.S. Army's involvement in the Pacific and beyond.

Tuesday to Saturday: 9:00 AM to 5:00 PM
Audio tours are available for rent, $5 each ($2.50 each for Society members).
Admission: Free; however, donations are always welcome. Parking: Validated parking for the U.S. Army Museum of Hawai'i is at the Fort DeRussy Parking Facilities. With validation, the fee is $2.00 for the first hour (or fraction thereof) and $1.25 for each additional hour (or fraction thereof). Please present your parking ticket to the receptionist for validation.

Getting there:

The Hawai'i Army Museum is located on the grounds of the Hale Koa Hotel and the Ft. DeRussy Recreation Center in Waikīkī.

Sites requiring base access I.D.

HICKAM AIR FORCE BASE – HOSPITAL POINT

The USS *Nevada* was the only battleship to get underway during the Pearl Harbor attacks, run aground at Hospital Point near the harbor's entrance in order to keep the narrow channel free of obstructions. If you are able to secure a boat tour of Pearl Harbor, you will most likely view this area at the edge of Hickam Air Force Base. From land, with a base I.D., you can view the memorial marker at Hickam. In addition, from the eastern tip of Ford Island you can look across the channel to Hospital Point.

NAVAL AIR MUSEUM BARBERS POINT

The mission of this small aviation museum is to preserve the U.S. Navy and Coast Guard aviation history of operations at Barber's Point. Several jets and helicopters are on display for visitors to view. Admittance is by appointment only.

Monday to Friday: 8:00 AM to 4:30 PM (by appointment)
Saturday to Sunday: (by appointment)

Getting there:

91-1299 Midway Dr., Honolulu, HI 96818
Phone (808) 682-3982

KĀNEʻOHE BAY PACIFIC WAR MEMORIAL

This Marine memorial is located at the entrance to the Marine Corps Base-Hawaii (MCBH) and has stunning views of Kāneʻohe Bay and of the scenic Koʻolau Mountain Range to the west. The memorial is a replica of one located at Newington, Connecticut, and pictures the famous Iwo Jima flag-raising photo taken by World War II news photographer Joe Rosenthal. Contrary to popular belief, the flag raising on Mt. Suribachi didn't signal victory that day over the Japanese forces on Iwo Jima, but it was an important rallying symbol that inspired American troops to win 31 days later a hard-fought victory on Iwo Jima.

Getting there:

Drive to the Windward-Side end of the H3 Freeway.

**Mutual Publishing offers other informative books
about Pearl Harbor, Ford Island,
and other historic military sites on O'ahu**

» Pearl Harbor Fact & Reference Book
by Terence McComas

If you consider yourself an expert on Pearl Harbor, an armchair historian, or if you are looking for a quick reference source on the Pearl Harbor attack, this book is a must.

ISBN-10: 0-935180-02-8 · ISBN-13: 978-0-935180-02-2
Trim size: 6 x 9 in. · Binding: Softcover · Page count: 132 · Retail: $11.95

» From Fishponds to Warships: Pearl Harbor –A Complete History
by Allan Seiden

A walk through this famous site from its presettlement days, when it was an uninhabited tropical lagoon, to the famous attack in 1941, and to the present, where it has become an American icon visited by millions every year.

Trim size: 11 x 9.125 in. · Page count: 128
Softcover ISBN-10: 1-56647-505-8 · ISBN-13: 978-1-56647-505-1 · Retail: $22.50
Hardcover ISBN-10: 1-56647-511-2 · ISBN-13: 978-1-56647-511-2 · Retail: $27.50

» Battleship Missouri
by Ronn Ronck

The USS *Missouri*, the last battleship built by the United States, ruled the seas when she fired her nine 16-inch guns. Ronn Ronck tells the full, exciting story of this floating fortress, from its christening by President Truman's daughter, Margaret, onward.

ISBN-10: 1-56647-252-0 · ISBN-13: 978-1-56647-252-4
Trim size: 8.5 x 11 in. · Binding: Softcover · Page count: 72 · Retail: $11.95

» Pearl Harbor in the Movies
by Ed Rampell and Luis I. Reyes

America's fascination with Pearl Harbor is eternal, and nowhere is it more evident than in film. In the sixty years since that fateful day in 1941, scores of movies have featured this infamous landmark.

ISBN-10: 1-56647-506-6 · ISBN-13: 978-1-56647-506-8
Trim size: 8.5 x 11 in. · Binding: Softcover · Page count: 160 · Retail: $16.95

» A History of Fort DeRussy:
U.S. Army Museum of Hawai'i
by Pierre Moulin

A comprehensive history of Fort DeRussy, the site of the U.S. Army Museum of Hawai'i. Today, the museum's galleries document the U.S. military presence in Hawai'i, honor the soldiers of the 442nd Regimental Combat Team, and commemorate the men and women fighting our current wars.

ISBN-10: 1-56647-850-2 · ISBN-13: 978-1-56647-850-2
Trim size: 8.5 x 11 in. · Binding: Softcover · Page count: 80 · Retail: $17.95

» A History of Punchbowl
by Pierre Moulin

A History of Punchbowl tells the story of the place from its earliest days as a site of ancient rituals to when it was a fort for the Hawaiian Kingdom and a gun battery during the uncertain years of the Second World War.

ISBN-10: 0-9755210-0-4 · ISBN-13: 978-0-9755210-0-7
Trim size: 8.5 x 11 in. · Binding: Softcover · Page count: 96 · Retail: $19.95

Find these titles and more at
www.mutualpublishing.com

ABOUT THE AUTHORS

Meloni Courtway has been a freelance writer for over a decade working for Gannett and the *New York Times* newspapers as well as blogging about the various places where she has lived. She is especially connected to Pearl Harbor because her father-in-law and grandfather-in-law are retired Navy sailors. She is inspired by the unique and sometimes untold heroic stories found at Pearl Harbor, Ford Island, and beyond. Her husband, Edgar Courtway, is a Chief Petty Officer in the United States Coast Guard, stationed at Communication Station Honolulu since 2012.

Chris Cook, the author of *The New Kaua'i Movie Book*, the literary collection *A Kaua'i Reader,* and other books dealing with Hawai'i's past, is a graduate of the University of Hawai'i. During his college years, he worked on projects located within O'ahu's military installations including Pearl Harbor, and Ford Island, where he and his co-workers rode the Ford Island ferry to and from their job site. As a reporter at Kaua'i's *The Garden Island* newspaper, he was a submariner for a day aboard an Ohio-Class nuclear submarine out of the Pearl Harbor sub base.

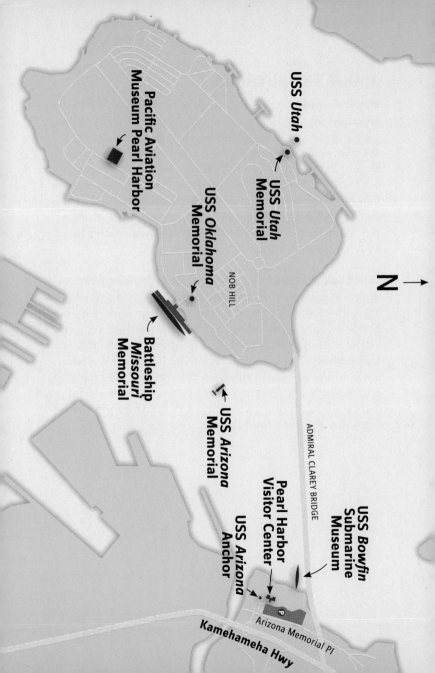

USS *Utah*

Pacific Aviation
Museum Pearl Harbor

USS *Utah*
Memorial

USS *Oklahoma*
Memorial

NOB HILL

N →

Battleship
Missouri
Memorial

USS *Arizona*
Memorial

ADMIRAL CLAREY BRIDGE

USS *Bowfin*
Submarine
Museum

Pearl Harbor
Visitor Center

USS *Arizona*
Anchor

Arizona Memorial Pl

Kamehameha Hwy